PARAGRAPH DEVELOPMENT

A Guide for Students of English as a Second Language

MARTIN L. ARNAUDET
MARY ELLEN BARRETT

English Language Institute
The American University
Washington, D.C.

PRENTICE-HALL, INC.
Englewood Cliffs, New Jersey 07632

Library of Congress Cataloging in Publication Data

ARNAUDET, MARTIN L
    Paragraph development.

    Includes index.
    1. English language—Text-books for foreigners.
2. English language—Paragraphs.   I. Barrett, Mary
Ellen, joint author.   II. Title.
PE112828.A67   808′.042   80-24575
ISBN 0-13-648618-5

© 1981 by Prentice-Hall, Inc., Englewood Cliffs, N.J. 07632

Printed in the United States of America

10   9   8   7   6

Editorial production/supervision by Diane Lange
Cover design by Jayne Conte
Manufacturing buyer: Harry P. Baisley

PRENTICE-HALL INTERNATIONAL, INC., *London*
PRENTICE-HALL OF AUSTRALIA PTY. LIMITED, *Sydney*
PRENTICE-HALL OF CANADA, LTD., *Toronto*
PRENTICE-HALL OF INDIA PRIVATE LIMITED, *New Delhi*
PRENTICE-HALL OF JAPAN, INC., *Tokyo*
PRENTICE-HALL OF SOUTHEAST ASIA PTE. LTD., *Singapore*
WHITEHALL BOOKS LIMITED, *Wellington, New Zealand*

CONTENTS

6
SUPPORTING TOPIC SENTENCES
Comparison and Contrast

7
DEFINITION

8
FROM PARAGRAPH
TO COMPOSITION

FOREWORD

Each year teachers of English as a Second Language generate mountains of teaching materials to meet immediate and specific needs of their students. Many of these materials are very good; others are not. However, whether they are good or not so good, they are all relegated to the "archives" of teacher-generated materials, to be seen again only when offices are moved and desks cleaned out.

With the regularity of total eclipses, however, the Muses smile favorably, and the need for specific materials which the teacher feels is also felt by the program in which he works and by the profession in general. The materials presented here are the result of one of those total eclipses: Dr. Arnaudet and Mrs. Barrett, the English Lanugage Institute, and the profession in general have felt the need for materials to bridge the gap between sentence and composition. These materials have been developed, tested, revised, and retested over a period of three years, not only at The American University but also at several other universities, and they do fill the gap. A student can now systematically be brought from the perfect sentence through the paragraph to the composition in a series of logical and practical steps that take the mystery out of developing and writing a paragraph.

It is indeed a very pleasant thing to see two dedicated teachers recognized for years of hard work which have culminated in the publication of their materials. I am sure your students will benefit from this text as much as our students have.

Robert P. Fox, Ph.D.
Director, English Language Institute
The American University

PREFACE

Paragraph Development is an integrated guide for high intermediate to advanced learners of English. It focuses on the physical paragaph as a basic unit of composition common to most forms of academic, business, professional, and general-purpose writing. It is designed to be flexible enough to be used as a writing component in an intensive or semi-intensive program or as an independent writing course. The book is based on the theory that if a student is able to write a unified, coherent paragraph, transferring this skill to full composition writing will not be difficult. The approach in each chapter is direct and functional: a model is provided and graphically explained; then the student is asked to imitate the model.

ORGANIZATION OF THE MATERIAL

Units One and Two deal with limiting and supporting topic sentences. In Unit One, students are directed from identifying elements which limit a topic to writing their own topic sentences. In Unit Two, they are asked to analyze, through diagrams, how supporting material (examples, details, anecdotes, and statistics) relates directly to the topic sentence and thus creates unity within the paragraph.

Units Three through Six deal with the rhetorical patterns most commonly found in expository writing (Enumeration, Process, Chronology, Cause and

Effect, and Comparison and Contrast). Fictional narration has purposely been omitted as primarily a literary device. Each paragraph type is introduced with a model, followed by graphic analysis and controlled exercises which ultimately lead to a free writing assignment. Although this book is *not* intended as a grammar text, some structures are reviewed in these units as they apply to the specific type of paragraph being discussed.

Unit Seven treats Definition not as a rhetorical device in and of itself, but rather as a kind of writing which often employs a variety of rhetorical devices.

Unit Eight is concerned with transferring the patterns of paragraph development to full composition writing.

SPECIAL FEATURES

1. Neither the model paragraphs nor the exercises have been simplified or edited for non-native speakers. Because the text is intended for use at a number of levels and in a variety of programs, items within exercises which are more difficult because of vocabulary, content, or length have been starred (°) to indicate to both teacher and student that they are more challenging.

2. In each unit, a "Now Ask Yourself" review exercise follows the presentation of any new material. These exercises force the student to integrate what he has previously learned, to reinterpret it, and to apply it to the task at hand. This spiraling of concepts ensures greater student involvement and conceptual mastery of the material.

3. The paraphrasing exercises in Units Three through Seven provide the students with the opportunity to practice sentences typical of each pattern of development before incorporating these patterns into free writing assignments.

4. Charts and diagrams are used to illustrate relationships within paragraphs—and finally within longer pieces of discourse—and to provide a visual, structural focus. We have chosen to call them *paragraph analysis* exercises. They are, in point of fact, reading exercises of the "information transfer" type, proceeding from the verbal to the visual. These charts and diagrams can easily be adapted to an *academic outline format* at the discretion of the teacher.

5. "Information transfer" exercises proceeding in the other direction—i.e. from the visual to the verbal—take the student from an analytical/reading stage into controlled writing. In each case, the student is asked to take facts which have been presented in a skeletal way (diagrams, time lines, pictures, etc.) and to express them in written form using the pattern being studied. We feel that this is a particularly important and useful skill for a student to acquire before attempting unstructured composition.

ACKNOWLEDGMENTS

During the preparation of this book, we have become indebted to many people—students and colleagues, present and former, who have used this text experimentally, as well as reviewers and friends—for their many helpful comments and for their encouragement. We are particularly grateful to Robert P. Fox, Director, and Mary Ann G. Hood, Associate Director, for allowing us the time and the full resources of the English Language Institute in our efforts to produce this book.

Special thanks go to Carol Power of the University of South Florida for her encouragement and support.

MLA
MEB
Washington, D.C.

1

THE TOPIC SENTENCE

Paragraph Unity

THE PARAGRAPH

In written form, English is divided into *paragraphs* to distinguish one main idea from other main ideas. The paragraph is the *basic unit of composition.*

REMEMBER THIS
1. A paragraph is a group of sentences which develop one central idea.
2. The central idea is usually stated in a *topic sentence.*
3. Every sentence in the paragraph must help the development of the topic sentence.

INDENTATION

The first sentence of a paragraph is always *indented* so that the reader will know that a new subject—or a different aspect of the same subject—is being dealt with. The writer does this by leaving a blank space at the beginning of the paragraph. The student should think of indentation as simply *another kind of punctuation.* Just as a sentence ends with a period (.), so each new paragraph begins with an *indentation.*

If you are not already familiar with the idea of indentation, be sure to study the following diagram very carefully:

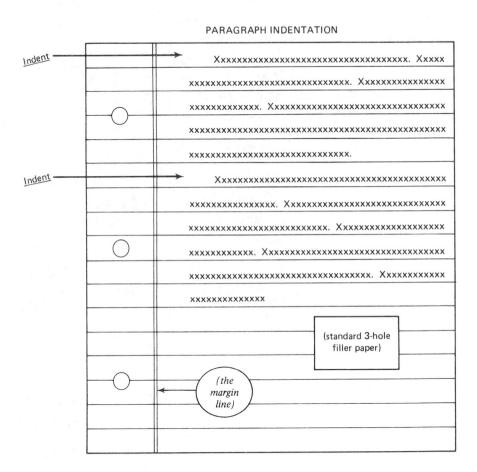

PARAGRAPH INDENTATION

LENGTH

A paragraph may vary in length. Some paragraphs are quite short; others are extremely long. Most paragraphs have more than three sentences in them and usually have between one hundred and two hundred words.

1. What is a paragraph? _____

   _____

2. What is the proper "punctuation" for a paragraph? _____

   Where is it located in the paragraph? _____

3. How long should a paragraph be? _____

TOPIC VS. TOPIC SENTENCE

The first sentence of a paragraph is usually called the *topic sentence.* You have no doubt noticed in your reading of certain English texts that it is possible to place the topic sentence at the *end* of the paragraph (as a kind of conclusion), or even in the *middle* (as a kind of link between the two parts). It is even possible not to have a topic sentence at all; in this case, we say that the topic sentence is *implied* or *suggested.* You should be aware of these possibilities when you read; otherwise, you might miss the point which the author is trying to make. When you write, however, remember that a topic sentence placed at the beginning of a paragraph is the clearest kind of paragraph organization—simple, effective, easy for you to manage, and easy for your reader to understand.

What makes a good topic sentence?

The most important thing to remember at this point is the following: in a topic sentence, always try to make a *statement* about your topic which *limits* it to a certain extent:

Topic Sentence = TOPIC + LIMITING STATEMENT

Take, for example, the general topic of *soccer.* There are too many things to say about soccer to put into a single paragraph. Therefore, your problem as a writer consists in deciding how you want to write about soccer. In other words, you need to *limit* your discussion.

One good way to limit your topic is to place *key words or phrases* in the topic sentence. These words or phrases will let the reader know how you are going to discuss the topic. These words or phrases are sometimes called "controlling words or phrases," since they control the organization of the paragraph. In a paragraph on soccer, for example, they will immediately indicate to the reader that you plan to do *one* of several things:

Discuss the history of soccer

Compare it with another sport

Describe its difficulty

Explain the rules of the game

How do you limit a topic in a topic sentence? There are many ways, but below you will find a list of the most common. Once you understand these examples, you will find it much easier to write a carefully controlled topic sentence:

Topic	Statement Which Limits the Topic
1. Soccer	is now played in the United States. (geographical location)
2. Soccer	has become more popular within the last five years. (time or period of time)
3. Soccer	is a physically demanding sport. (a certain aspect)
4. Soccer and football	have a great deal in common. (showing similarities)
5. Soccer	is more dangerous than tennis. (showing differences)
6. A soccer player	can receive various kinds of penalties (a number of things; a list) during a game.
7. The World Cup Soccer Champion- ship Games	create interest from soccer fans all over (effect) the world.
8. Soccer	is dangerous for several reasons. (cause; reason)

 NOW ASK YOURSELF

1. Where does a topic sentence usually come in a paragraph? _____

2. Where else can it come? _____

3. What should a writer always try to do to his topic in a topic sentence?

_____

4. What are eight kinds of statements which a writer can use to limit his topic?

a. _____   e. _____

b. _____   f. _____

c. _____   g. _____

d. _____   h. _____

EXERCISE 1-1
Identifying Categories Which
Limit Topic Sentences

Directions: Notice the controlling words and phrases which have been underlined in the example sentence. They have also been identified as to type. Notice also that it is possible to have *more than one* category in a single topic sentence. After you have studied the example, do the same for the remaining sentences. Choose from the eight categories on p. 4:

1. Place
2. Time
3. Aspect
4. Similarities
5. Differences
6. Number
7. Effect
8. Cause

1. Soccer has become increasingly popular in the United States in the last ten years.   (aspect)   (place)   (time)
2. Team sports develop an athlete's sense of fair play.
   (   )
3. Libraries have three basic kinds of materials.
   (   )
4. Women are paid less for equal work than men in certain companies.
   (   )   (   )

5. Pollution <u>has caused</u> <u>three major problems</u> <u>in our town</u> <u>in the last 5 years.</u>
   (   ) (   ) (   ) (   )

6. Air travel <u>is more convenient than</u> train travel <u>for at least three reasons.</u>
   (   )   (   ) (   )

EXERCISE 1-2
Guided Practice in
Limiting General Topics

Directions: Write a topic sentence for each of the topics listed below. The topic is given. Your job is to *limit* it in the way(s) which have been suggested. Follow the example.

1. Topic: John F. Kennedy (aspect) (place)
   <u>John F. Kennedy was the first Catholic president elected in the United</u>
   <u>States.</u>   (aspect)   (place)

2. Topic: registration at a large university (aspect) (differences)

   _____

3. Topic: shopping for food (place) (aspect) (differences)

   _____

4. Topic: smoking (effect)

   _____

5. Topic: American food (differences)

   _____

6. Topic: study habits (number) (effect)

   _____

EXERCISE 1-3
Limiting General Topics

Directions: Below you will find several different topics, all of which are too broad (i.e., too general) to be used as they are. You should limit them. For each topic, write *two* completely different topic sentences which might serve as topic sentences of two different paragraphs. In parentheses below the sentences, indicate what categories you have used. Follow the example.

1. Topic: soccer
   a. There are many reasons for soccer's increased popularity in the United
      States. (number) (reason)   (aspect)   (place)
   b. Latin Americans generally prefer soccer to football.
              (place)   (differences)

2. Topic: the role of women

   a. _____

   b. _____

3. Topic: religion in modern society

   a. _____

   b. _____

4. Topic: war

   a. _____

   b. _____

5. Topic: problems between generations

   a. _____

   b. _____

6. Topic: crime

   a. _____

   b. _____

EXERCISE 1-4
Limiting the Same General Topic

Directions: Take the following topic and write five (5) completely different
topic sentences based on it. Refer back to the list of categories if necessary.

Topic: foreign students in the United States

1. _____

2. _____

3. _____

4. _____

5. _____

PARAGRAPH UNITY

Remember that besides the topic sentence, a paragraph includes several other sentences which in some way contribute to or *support* the idea in the topic sentence. In other words, all these sentences must be *related to* the topic and must therefore refer back to the topic sentence. Notice the arrows in the following diagram:

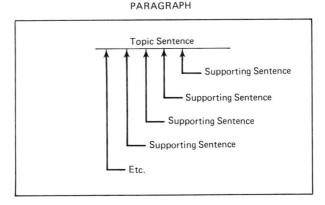

It is possible, of course, that some sentences may be directly related to the preceding supporting sentences (i.e., they provide examples, details, or further explanation):

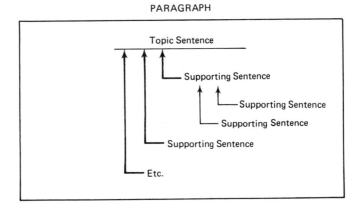

 *NOW ASK YOURSELF*

1. What must all supporting sentences do? _____

   _____

2. What is illustrated by the arrows in the two previous diagrams?

   (the first diagram) _____

   _____

   (the second diagram) _____

   _____

If a paragraph does all this—that is, 1) if it announces its main idea in the topic sentence, and 2) if all the supporting sentences contribute to the reader's understanding of the main idea—we say that a paragraph is *unified*, or that it has *unity*. If the paragraph fails to do this, we say that it lacks unity.

Study the following paragraph. It *lacks* unity. Before reading the explanation which follows, can you figure out why it is not unified? (The sentences have been numbered only to make the discussion easier. Do not number sentences like this when you write a paragraph!)

> [1]There are two main reasons why I have decided to attend Bingston University next year. [2]Applying to a college is a terribly complicated process. [3]Some of my friends chose colleges for very bad reasons. [4]John has never been to college. [5]I've met his grandfather, and he still has an incredibly sharp mind for a man of his age. [6]Susan chose a university because the food in the region was said to be quite good. [7]Susan is really not too clever, I suppose, so I shouldn't criticize her. [8]Actually, I think it was her father who made the choice for her.

Did you notice that *none* of the above sentences actually discusses the topic which was announced in the topic sentence? The paragraph was supposed to be about the writer's *two main reasons* for choosing Bingston University. However, he never actually tells us. He writes about many unrelated things— his friend John, John's grandfather, his friend Susan, Susan's stupidity, etc.— *but not his* **two reasons for choosing Bingston University!** If we wanted to show this by means of a diagram of the paragraph, we might do it this way:

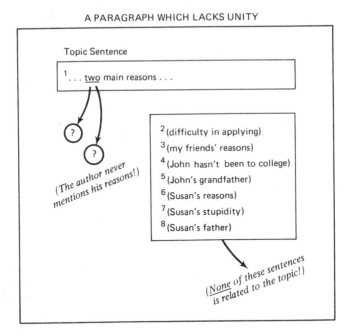

A PARAGRAPH WHICH LACKS UNITY

Topic Sentence

1 . . . <u>two</u> main reasons . . .

? ?

(The author never mentions his reasons!)

2 (difficulty in applying)
3 (my friends' reasons)
4 (John hasn't been to college)
5 (John's grandfather)
6 (Susan's reasons)
7 (Susan's stupidity)
8 (Susan's father)

(<u>None</u> of these sentences is related to the topic!)

If we wanted to keep the same topic sentence and rewrite the paragraph in a more unified fashion, we might end up with something like this:

¹There are two main reasons why I have decided to attend Bingston University next year. ²First of all, there is the question of money: Bingston's tuition is reasonable, and I don't even have to pay it all at once. ³This is very important, since my father is not a rich man. ⁴With Bingston's "deferred payment plan," my father will be able to pay my tuition without too much difficulty. ⁵The second reason is the fine education which I feel I will receive there in agriculture, my chosen field. ⁶It is a well-known fact that Bingston hires only the finest professors in its Agriculture Department. ⁷Moreover, the university requires all agricultural students to gain practical experience by working on farms in the area while they are still going to school.

This is what a diagram of the above paragraph would look like:

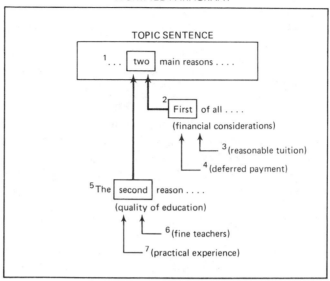

A UNIFIED PARAGRAPH

TOPIC SENTENCE

¹... two main reasons ....

² First of all ....
(financial considerations)
³ (reasonable tuition)
⁴ (deferred payment)

⁵ The second reason ....
(quality of education)
⁶ (fine teachers)
⁷ (practical experience)

Notice that in the rewritten paragraph, the writer gives us *both* his reasons and comments on both of them. Nothing is extra. Nothing is irrelevant to the topic announced in the topic sentence. *The paragraph is unified.* This means that the reader will have no trouble quickly understanding what the writer is trying to say.

 NOW ASK YOURSELF

1. How are sentences 2 and 5 related to the topic sentence? _____

_____

2. How are sentences 3 and 4 related to sentence 2?_____

_____

3. How are sentences 6 and 7 related to sentence 5? _____

_____

4. How are all these relationships indicated in the diagram? _____

_____

5. Why is the rewritten paragraph better than the original one? _____

EXERCISE 1-5
Identifying Irrelevant Sentences

Directions: The following paragraphs contain sentences which are not directly related to the main ideas of those paragraphs. Draw a line through the irrelevant sentence(s) of each paragraph. Then circle the *key words or phrases* in the topic sentence. Be prepared to explain why you think the sentences are irrelevant.

1.   ¹Different people spend their weekends in different ways. ²Some enjoy going to the mountains to hike, ski, or just relax. ³Water skiing is much more difficult than snow skiing. ⁴Others prefer going to the beach to enjoy the seashore activities and to get a suntan. ⁵Some of these people work very hard during the week; others have rather relaxing jobs. ⁶Still others like to relax by staying home and reading a good book.

2.   ¹Ever since the time of the Greeks, drama has played an important role in men's lives. ²The Greek tragedies and comedies were a central part of the life of the citizens of ancient Greece. ³During the Middle Ages, Bible stories were acted out in churches, and wandering companies of players performed in the streets. ⁴William Shakespeare lived during the Elizabethan period. ⁵The English language has changed somewhat since Shakespeare's time. ⁶In modern times, drama is brought directly into people's homes through the magic of television. ⁷Television also offers people such things as quiz and variety shows.

3.   ¹Innovations, whether practical or aesthetic, are often resisted by the general population. ²When the early experimenters in the field of aviation began their work, there were many who said, "If God had wanted man to fly, He would have given him wings." ³The Wright brothers made the first powered flights in a heavier-than-air craft in 1903 at Kitty Hawk, North Carolina. ⁴Even today there are many who strongly object to modern art and music as being nothing more than "splashes of paint and honking horns." ⁵The painter Picasso's well-known masterpiece "The Three Musicians" is done primarily in blues and browns.

4.   [1]Zoos are popular with all children. [2]They are able to see examples of wildlife from all continents. [3]In wildlife preserves in Africa, the animals wander about freely without fear of being captured. [4]Perhaps the favorite spot in a zoo is the elephant cage. [5]There the elephants entertain the children by spraying themselves with their trunks and doing various tricks. [6]The children are especially delighted when an elephant takes peanuts from them with his trunk.

5.   [1]Editorials differ from other kinds of news stories. [2]In most regular news stories, it is assumed that no personal opinions are being represented. [3]Newspaper writers are supposed to present the facts of each story in a straightforward, unbiased fashion. [4]Statistics reveal that over sixty-one million newspapers are sold every day in this country. [5]The purpose of the editorial page, of course, is to allow the editors to give their personal opinions. [6]Here is where they tell readers what they think about an issue—who is at fault, who has done a good job, or how a situation could be improved. [7]It is no wonder, then, that Thomas Jefferson was once led to remark that he could more easily accept newspapers without government than government without newspapers.

6.   [1]In order to find a suitable apartment, you must follow a very systematic approach. [2]First, you must decide which neighborhood would be most convenient for you. [3]Then you must determine how much rent your budget will allow. [4]Utility bills for houses average between $100 and $150 per month. [5]Your next step is to check the classified ads in the newspapers. [6]If you do not plan to buy furniture, you should check under "Apartments for rent—furnished." [7]Otherwise, check under "Apartments for rent—unfurnished." [8]In either case, however, be sure to check these ads regularly, since new listings appear each day. [9]After you have telephoned the apartments which seem likely choices, you must begin your long journey to inspect each one of them.

EXERCISE 1-6
Identifying Suitable Topic Sentences

Directions: After reading each of the following paragraphs, select the most suitable topic sentence from the three choices following it, and write the sentence which you have selected in the blank. Then try to explain why each of the other two items is not appropriate. Follow the example. Possible reasons for not choosing an item might be that

It is too general;

It is too specific;

It is not a complete grammatical sentence;

It does not relate to the supporting sentences.

I.   There are some minor differences between American and British spelling. Where Britons end certain words with -se, Americans usually end the same words with -ce (British *practise* vs. American *practice*); the reverse is sometimes true, too (British *defence* vs. American *defense*). Notice also the British preference for final -re over the American -er (*metre* vs. *meter*). Finally, most Americans consider *neighbor* a correct spelling, but a Briton characteristically adds a *u* and spells the word *neighbour*.

Choose a Topic Sentence

A. British and American English are not the same.

B. There are some minor differences between American and British spelling.

C. The endings of British and American words are not the same.

Defend Your Choice

1. I did not choose letter A because it is too general (some aspects are not the the same; others are).

2. I did not choose letter C because it is too general (some endings are not the same).

II.   _____

_____. The operation of both can be thought of as being divided into three phases: *input, processing,* and *output.* In the case of the computer, the information which is fed into the machine—the data—is the input; the internal operations of the machine constitute the processing; and the result—usually a printout—is called the output. The telephone, too, acts on information presented to it and produces a result. The input is the actual dialing of the number. The switching system which locates the number can be considered the processing phase. Finally, the telephone rings on the other end of the line, indicating that the call has been completed; this constitutes the output.[1]

[1]Adapted from John C. Keegel, *The Language of Computer Programming in English* (New York: Regents Publishing Co., Inc., 1976), p. 4.

Choose a Topic Sentence

    A. Both the computer and the telephone are helpful inventions.

    B. Computer terminology, such as *input* and *output*, is frequently used in other contexts.

    C. Despite apparent differences, the operation of the computer and the telephone have much in common.

Defend Your Choice

    1. I did not choose letter ___ because _____

    _____

    2. I did not choose letter ___ because _____

    _____

III.   _____

_____. The jack is a portable device for raising the car. It operates by means of force being applied to a level on which the car is balanced. The lug wrench is a tool with a fixed "jaw" for gripping the lug (the type of screw used to hold a tire in place). It has a long handle so that it is effective in turning the lug, either to tighten or to loosen it. These are the only two tools necessary to change a tire. They are usually found in the trunk of the car and are kept there at all times so that the motorist can use them, should he have a flat tire.

Choose a Topic Sentence

    A. Flat tires constitute a serious problem for the motorist.

    B. How to change a flat tire.

    C. Only two tools are considered standard equipment on new U.S. automobiles.

Defend Your Choice

    1. I did not choose letter ___ because _____

    _____

2. I did not choose letter __ because _____

_____

IV. _____

_____. The first one is the small
pocket dictionary. Dictionaries of this type are usually only abridg-
ments of earlier, more comprehensive dictionaries. The definitions
found in a pocket dictionary are usually rather sketchy, and few or
no example sentences are given to help the foreign student understand *how* the word is actually used in a sentence. Equally inade-
quate is the bilingual dictionary (Thai-English, Spanish-English, Rus-
sian-English, etc.). This type of dictionary is often based on the idea
of making word-for-word translations, a notion which shows no
understanding of the idiomatic nature of all languages. Moreover,
bilingual dictionaries are often hastily and sloppily compiled, as well
as hopelessly out of date even before they are published.

Choose a Topic Sentence

A. A number of dictionaries are inappropriate for foreign students.
B. Some dictionaries aren't comprehensive enough.
C. The worst kind of dictionaries.

Defend Your Choice

1. I did not choose letter __ because _____

_____

2. I did not choose letter __ because _____

_____

V. _____

_____. For one thing, more
than ten percent of all "senior citizens" in the United States are
extremely poor. As a matter of fact, recent statistics suggest that
approximately one-seventh of all people over the age of sixty-five

live below the poverty level. Aged people also have more health problems than younger people. A third area for concern stems from the fact that public transportation has not been designed with old people in mind; their activities are often limited to whatever is within walking distance. And finally, there is the separation from family, which causes loneliness. Many older people live by themselves (this is particularly true of widows and divorced women). And then there are the "forgotten five percent," the older people who have been institutionalized—that is, sent to "old age homes" (sometimes called "nursing homes") by families who either cannot or will not take care of them.

Choose a Topic Sentence:

A. Some of the older people in the United States face a number of serious problems.

B. Old age problems.

C. Retirement homes in the United States are a disgrace.

Defend Your Choice

1. I did not choose letter __ because _____

_____

2. I did not choose letter __ because _____

_____

VI.   _____

_____. Infants usually satisfy this very basic need in the course of an ordinary day spent with their parents (feeding, kissing, bathing, etc.). However, if a baby is neglected or even mistreated by being deprived of touch, his development will suffer on all levels—physical, intellectual, and emotional. Some children have even been known to die from this lack of tactile stimulation; it is thought by many doctors that many unexplained "crib deaths" are directly related to lack of touch and its various consequences. Children given out for adoption at a tender age and placed in poorly run orphanages, children brought up by unaffectionate parents, and children whose parents touch them only to beat them—all these types of children run the risk of never reaching their potential as fully developed adults.

Choose a Topic Sentence

    A. Babies interacting daily with their parents.

    B. Physical contact is an important factor in an infant's overall development.

    C. Many children are not properly taken care of by their parents.

Defend Your Choice

1. I did not choose letter __ because _____

    _____

2. I did not choose __ letter because _____

    _____

EXERCISE 1-7
Supplying Appropriate Topic Sentences

Directions: The topic sentences of each of the following paragraphs have been omitted. After a *careful* reading, write an appropriate sentence for each. Notice that the *general topics* of these paragraphs are the same as those in the previous exercise.

1.   _____

_____. When you have removed the hubcap from the wheel which has the flat, the jack should be correctly placed so as to be able to lift the car off the ground. Now you are ready to jack up the car high enough for the tire to *clear* the ground. After you have done that, carefully loosen the nuts that hold the tire and rim in place; the tool which you use to do that is called a *lug wrench*. Remove the tire and put the spare tire in place. Now you are ready to put the nuts back on the wheel and tighten them well with the lug wrench. All that remains is to replace the hubcap.

2.   _____

_____. The one most people are familiar

with is the "desk dictionary," sometimes referred to as a *general-purpose dictionary*. Another kind is the *pronouncing dictionary*, which is concerned with a word's pronunciation more than with its meaning. A third type is the *bilingual dictionary*, which lists the words in one language and attempts to give equivalent meanings in another language. Other types include *technical dictionaries, special-purpose dictionaries*, and *scholarly dictionaries*.

3. _____

_____. Under this new system, the customer's monthly telephone bill includes specific information for each long-distance call: the date and time of each call, the rate charged per minute (based on the company's discount system), the length of time the call took, the number and place called, whether the call was direct-dialed or operator-assisted, and the amount charged for the call. As each call is placed, all of this information is fed into a computer and programmed onto each customer's billing card, thus simplifying and clarifying the entire billing process. The Bell Telephone Company hopes that its new billing procedure will reduce the number of inquiries and free its employees to do work which computers are not yet able to perform.

4. _____

_____. To be eligible for these benefits, a person must be sixty-five years old and must have been participating in the Social Security system for a certain number of years. First, *retirement benefits* provide a worker with a monthly income ranging from $230 to almost $490, depending on his salary when he was working and the number of years he paid into the system. The second benefit is *survivors' benefits*, a kind of life insurance which provides a deceased worker's widow and children under eighteen with monthly cash payments based on what the worker would have received as retirement benefits. A third category is *disability benefits*. Workers, their widows, and their children under eighteen may be eligible for monthly payments if they are unable to work because of severe physical or mental illness. Finally, most people over sixty-five who are receiving disability payments are also entitled to *Medicare*. This insurance protection helps to pay hospital costs and covers partial payment for other medical expenses, such as doctor bills and medication.

°5.   _____

_____. We often use this sense, for example, to describe how we have dealt with a person or a situation. If we have been successful, we feel that we have "the right touch" or "the magic touch" or that we have "come to grips" with the person or the situation; if unsuccessful, we may feel that we have "lost touch" or "lost our grip" or are "out of touch" with reality. We also use this sense to describe a variety of emotional responses and states. We "feel" happy, sad, or depressed. In fact, we use the same kind of language to judge a person's very capacity for these kinds of emotions: we speak of a "sensitive" person or of an "unfeeling" person; even the adjectives "warm" and "cold" are related to the sense of touch. When we love a person, we have that person "under our skin"; when we hate him, he "makes our skin crawl."

°From this point on in the text, some items in some exercises will be marked with an asterisk to indicate that, because of vocabulary, length, or subject matter, they are more challenging.

2

SUPPORTING TOPIC SENTENCES

Examples, Details, Anecdotes, Facts and Statistics

Once you have limited your subject by writing a good topic sentence, you must next *develop* that subject so that the reader thoroughly understands what you mean to say. When you are speaking, you do this unconsciously, often by repeating yourself in different words and by using *gestures* and *facial expressions*. In writing *you cannot make use of these auditory and visual aids*, so you must think and plan carefully what you are going to write to ensure that your reader knows exactly what you mean.

There are many ways in which you can develop and clarify a topic sentence. In this chapter we will deal with four of these:

1. EXAMPLES
2. DETAILS
3. ANECDOTES
4. FACTS AND STATISTICS

EXAMPLES

An example is *a specific instance that explains an idea.*

Model Paragraph

Some of the most interesting words in English are the actual names of the people first involved in the activities conveyed by the meanings of the words. The word *boycott,* for instance, derives from the case of Sir Charles Boycott (1832–97), a land agent in Ireland who was ostracized by his tenants because he refused to lower the rents. Vidkun Quisling's name quickly became an infamous addition to the English language during World War II. He was a Norwegian politician who betrayed his country to the Nazis, and his name, *quisling,* is now synonymous with "traitor." Perhaps a more common example, at least among young people around the world, is *Levi's.* These popular blue jeans are named after Levi Strauss, the man who first manufactured them in San Francisco in 1850. Perhaps most omnipresent of all is the *sandwich,* named for the Fourth Earl of Sandwich (1718–92), who created this quick portable meal so that he would not have to leave the gambling table to eat. Other words in this unique category include *lynch, watt, davenport,* and *zeppelin.*

 NOW ASK YOURSELF

1. What words have been used in the model paragraph to introduce

   examples? _____
2. Are these kinds of words always necessary to introduce examples? (Compare the model paragraph which you have just read with paragraph 5,

   p. 20, in which many examples appear.)_____
3. Do you know the origins of these words?

   lynch _____

   watt _____

   davenport _____

   zeppelin _____

EXERCISE 2-1
Guided Analysis of the Use of Examples

Directions: Complete the analysis of the model paragraph by filling all blank spaces. Note that key phrases in the topic sentence have been circled.

ANALYSIS

> **Topic Sentence:** Some of the (most interesting words) in English are the actual (names of the people) first involved in the activities conveyed by the meanings of the words.

Example: boycott

Example: quisling

Example:

Example:

Example:

Example:

Example:

Example:

EXERCISE 2-2
Guided Analysis of the Use of Examples

Directions: Read and analyze the following paragraph.

In order to be considered a hero by his own and subsequent generations, a person must display extraordinary physical or intellectual powers. The physical hero—one who exhibits great strength to overcome monumental obstacles and emerge a victor—is found frequently in literature. Samson, although chained and bound, used his superhuman strength to destroy his enemies, the Philistines. Likewise, Dwight

Eisenhower, a more contemporary physical hero, surmounted over-whelming odds to organize the successful Allied invasion of "Fortress Europe" during World War II. A second heroic type is the intellectual, admired for his mental prowess and the way he uses it to the benefit of mankind. Leonardo DaVinci, with his studies of architecture, human anatomy, and engineering, in addition to his great artistic achievements, belongs to this second type. More recently, Albert Einstein, who not only made far-reaching contributions in the physical sciences, but also worked diligently towards achieving world peace, illustrates the intel-lectual hero.

ANALYSIS

Topic Sentence:

Example (Physical Hero): _____

Example (Physical Hero): _____

Example (   ): _____

Example (   ): _____

EXERCISE 2-3
Paragraph Writing: Examples

Directions: Write a paragraph on one of the following topics. Use *examples* to support your topic sentence. You may use the lines below as a work space for your first draft.

The Behavior of Someone in Love

Watching Television

Rearing Children

Owning a Car

Springtime

DETAILS

A detail is *a particular part or characteristic of a whole thing or a whole idea.* Details are frequently used in a description.

Model Paragraph

Landlords usually require a renter to sign a very complicated contract called a *lease*. It stipulates the length of time the person must stay in the apartment and the amount of rent he must pay. It can limit the number of people allowed to live in the apartment and restrict the renter from having pets. A lease may prohibit the renter from subletting and include a provision by which he is charged a certain amount of money if he breaks the contract. The agreement also includes the responsibilities of the landlord, such as providing adequate heat, garbage removal, and exterior maintenance of the apartment building.

EXERCISE 2-4
Guided Analysis of the Use of Details

Directions: Analyze the preceding paragraph by filling in the blanks below:

Topic Sentence: Landlords usually require a renter to sign a very (complicated contract) called (a lease.)

Detail: length of time _____

Detail: _____

Detail: _____

Detail: _____

Detail: _____

Detail: _____

Detail: _____

example: heat _____

example: _____

example: _____

Analyzing the Use of Details

Directions: Read and analyze the following paragraph. In your choice of major categories of details for the diagram, you might want to consider number of rows, method of replacement, maximum number of teeth, and shape of the bite.

Perhaps it is because of its terrifying and effective teeth that the shark has always been one of man's most hated and feared enemies. Located beneath its snout, the shark's mouth contains between four and six rows of teeth, but these may number up to twenty-four rows in some species. The teeth are embedded in the gums and gradually move forward as they are used. Eventually these large teeth drop out and are replaced by new teeth moving up from behind them. It is possible for one species of shark to produce up to 24,000 teeth over a ten-year period. This awesome dental equipment produces a jagged crescent-shaped bite.

ANALYSIS

EXERCISE 2-6
Information Transfer (Details)

Directions: Write a paragraph based on the following diagram. Use the topic sentence which has been given. Be careful: the details are given in *note form,* so you will have to convert them into grammatical sentences.

Topic Sentence: A newborn baby is really not very beautiful.

skin—discolored or wrinkled

eyes—frequently puffy and inflamed

shape of head—often distorted because of the difficult birth process

hair—either thick and unruly or nonexistent

movements—jerky and uncontrolled (muscles not yet developed)

_____

_____

_____

_____

_____

_____

_____

_____

_____

_____

_____

_____

_____

_____

_____

_____

_____

_____

_____

EXERCISE 2-7
Paragraph Writing: Details

Directions: Write a paragraph on one of the following topics. First, write a topic sentence in which you *clearly limit* the topic. Then support your topic sentence.

> The physical appearance of your favorite actor or actress
>
> The characteristics of a good nurse
>
> The features which you would like your next car to have
>
> Making a good sandwich

EXERCISE 2-8
Paragraph Writing: Details

In this assignment you will be asked to write a *description of one of your classmates.* Your teacher will give you time in class to study the physical appearance of the person and take notes. Then you should take the notes home and write the paragraph.

Do not concentrate on the person's clothing. Aim rather at describing the physical characteristics of the person in question (height, weight, complexion, hair color, facial and bodily features).

DON'T FORGET: Even in this kind of paragraph, the details you choose must support the topic sentence you have written.

ANECDOTES

An anecdote is *a short, entertaining account of some happening.* It is usually *personal.* It may be thought of as *a lengthy example.*

Model Paragraph

A film director's style is usually personal and recognizable, but every rule has its exception. Not long ago I was in a theatre watching Roman Polanski's *MacBeth.* Suddenly the action slowed considerably. A frightening red circle began moving outward from the center of the screen, engulfing first the actors and finally the entire scene. I was sitting on the edge of my seat, waiting for the next horror, which never came. It was not Polanski's terrifying style after all, but a fire in the film projector.

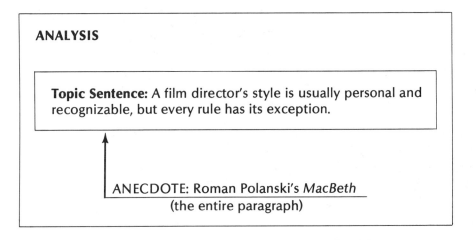

ANALYSIS

Topic Sentence: A film director's style is usually personal and recognizable, but every rule has its exception.

ANECDOTE: Roman Polanski's *MacBeth*
(the entire paragraph)

EXERCISE 2-9
Paragraph Writing: Anecdotes

Directions: Use an *anecdote* to support one of the following topic sentences:

A person's life can sometimes change overnight.

Computers create more problems than they solve.

Not knowing a language well can sometimes be embarrassing.

You know who your real friends are when you have a problem.

Love is not always happy.

FACTS AND STATISTICS

A fact is something which is objectively verifiable.

A statistic is *a numerical fact* which presents significant information about a given subject.

Model Paragraph

The term *population explosion* is usually applied to the rapid growth of the last three centuries. In the two hundred years from 1650 to 1850, world population doubled and reached its first billion. In the next eighty years, it doubled again, and by 1975, it had doubled once more to a total of 4 billion. By the year 2000, it is estimated that it will exceed 6 billion and possibly approach 7 billion unless there is a major reduction in birth rates or a major increase in death rates.

EXERCISE 2-10
Guided Analysis of the Use of Statistics

Directions: Analyze the model paragraph by filling in all blank spaces below.

ANALYSIS

Topic Sentence:

STATISTIC: 1650–1850; doubled, reached 1 billion

STATISTIC: _____

STATISTIC: _____

STATISTIC: _____

Directions: Read and analyze the following paragraph.

Exams apparently have a marked effect on the blood pressure of the students taking them. In a recent study, it was shown that the average student's blood pressure rose from 115/55 before the exam to 155/115 at the end of the exam. Ten minutes after the examination period had ended, the students' blood pressures were still quite high, averaging 150/110.

ANALYSIS

EXERCISE 2-12
Paragraph Writing:
Statistical Information Transfer

Directions: After studying the graph, write a paragraph using statistics from the graph to support the topic sentence which has been given.

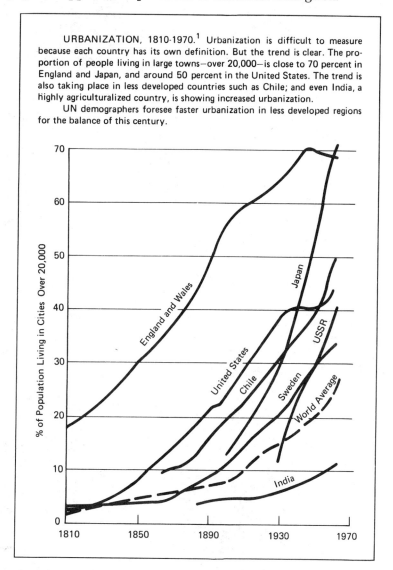

URBANIZATION, 1810-1970.[1] Urbanization is difficult to measure because each country has its own definition. But the trend is clear. The proportion of people living in large towns—over 20,000—is close to 70 percent in England and Japan, and around 50 percent in the United States. The trend is also taking place in less developed countries such as Chile; and even India, a highly agriculturalized country, is showing increased urbanization.

UN demographers foresee faster urbanization in less developed regions for the balance of this century.

[1]Population Reference Bureau, *The World Population Dilemma* (Washington, D.C.: Columbia Books, Inc., 1972). p. 19.

Urbanization has been increasing steadily in the United States since the early part of the nineteenth century. _____

_____

_____

_____

_____

_____

_____

_____

_____

_____

_____

_____

_____

_____

_____

_____

_____

_____

_____

_____

_____

3

SUPPORTING TOPIC SENTENCES

Enumeration

Thus far you have learned how to limit your subject in a clear, concise topic sentence and then to support it with examples, details, anecdotes, facts, and statistics. The next step is to arrange your supporting sentences in a logical and cohesive manner.

There are several ways in which this can be done. In this chapter we will deal with what is probably the most common method of paragraph development in English: *enumeration.*

ENUMERATION

What is *enumeration?*

In this type of paragraph development, a writer starts with a *general class,* then proceeds to break it down by *listing* some *or* all *of its members or parts.* If we wanted to show a diagram of the enumerative process, our diagram might look something like this:

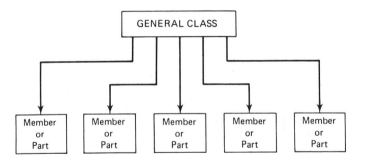

Model Paragraph

There are three basic kinds of materials that can be found in any good library. First, there are books on all subjects, both in English and in many other languages. These books are organized according to subject, title, and author in a central file called the card catalog. Books can generally be checked out of the library and taken home for a period of two to four weeks. Second, there are reference works, which include encyclopedias, dictionaries, bibliographies, atlases, etc., and which generally must be used in the library itself. Third, there are periodicals—magazines, newspapers, pamphlets—which are filed alphabetically in racks, or which have been microfilmed to conserve space. Like reference works, periodicals cannot usually be removed from the library.

Exercise 3-1
Guided Analysis of Enumeration

Directions: Analyze the model paragraph by filling in the empty parts of the chart below.

Topic Sentence: There are three basic kinds of materials that can be found in any good library.

KINDS OR TYPES	DESCRIPTION / EXAMPLES / ETC.
1. Books	On all subjects, in many languages; organized in the card catalog; can usually be checked out

KINDS OR TYPES	DESCRIPTION / EXAMPLES / ETC.
2. Reference works	

1. What are the key words in the topic sentence of the model paragraph?

   _____

2. What types of supportive information does the author use (examples, details, anecdotes, facts and statistics)? _____

   _____

3. How many kinds or types of library materials are talked about? _____

4. What is meant by enumeration? _____

ENUMERATORS

Notice the use of the word *kinds* in the preceding model paragraph. We will call this word an *enumerator* since it helps us show the reader exactly what we are listing or enumerating. In the model paragraph, it is *kinds of materials*. Remember that enumerators are valuable key words. You should try to put them in topic sentences of enumerative paragraphs. This will help you to organize your paragraphs more clearly; it will also help the reader to follow your train of thought more easily.

Writers frequently wish to make a list of other things besides *kinds* or *types*. They may, for example, want to talk about

Classes

Parts

Elements

Factors

Characteristics

Aspects

Divisions

Subdivisions

Categories

LISTING SIGNALS

When making a list, people often use *numerals* (e.g., 1, 2, 3, etc.) to indicate the various items in the list. A simple list of this kind could be made for the model paragraph on library materials:

Kinds of library materials found in most good libraries:

1. Books

2. Reference works

3. Periodicals

In most formal writing, however, a list is usually not made with numerals.° The items are indicated by what we call *listing signals*. The author of the model paragraph has used three of these listing signals: *First, . . . ; Second, . . . ; Third, ...* There are two main groups of listing signals in English. You should become very familiar with the words in these two groups:

GROUP 1

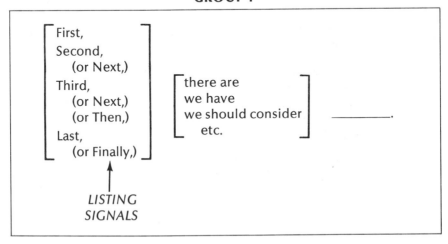

°A major exception to this is *scientific* and *technical* English, where it is common to find lists with a numeral before each item on the list.

GROUP 2

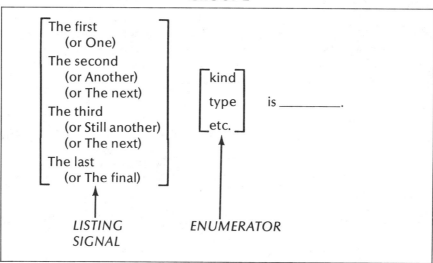

NOW ASK YOURSELF

1. What is the difference between an enumerator and a listing signal?

    _____

    _____

2. What is another way to say each of the following?

    (Last,) _____

    (The final kind) _____

    (Another kind) _____

    (Next,) _____

3. What element does a Group 2 sentence have that a Group 1 sentence

    does not? _____

GROUP 1 VS. GROUP 2: SENTENCE STRUCTURE

There is one thing that you *must* remember. The words in Group 1 take a *different sentence structure* from the words in Group 2. Let's take a sentence from the model paragraph on library materials and illustrate this difference, which is really a very simple one:

Group 1:	First,	there are	books.

Group 2:	The first kind	$\begin{bmatrix} \text{is} \\ \text{consists of} \end{bmatrix}$	books.

Note that a full sentence follows the listing signals from Group 1. Notice also that in Group 2, the listing signal and enumerator are the subject of the sentence. These differences, although simple, are *very important!*

EXERCISE 3-2
Paraphrasing Listing Signals

Directions: Rewrite each of the following sentences in three (3) ways, choosing words from *both* groups of listing signals. *Circle the enumerator* if you have used one.

1. Still another kind is periodicals.

    a. The next (kind) is periodicals.

    b. _____

    c. _____

2. Last, there are reference works.

    a. _____

    b. _____

    c. _____

EXERCISE 3-3
Supplying Listing Signals

Directions: Write listing signals for the following paragraph. Circle the enumerator in the topic sentence.

Most middle-class Americans use four main distances, or *zones,* in their business and social relations; each of these distances has a near and a far phase and is accompanied by a change in the volume of the voice. _____ intimate distance, which varies from direct physical contact to a distance of six to eighteen inches, and which is used for our most private activities—caressing another person or comforting a crying child. _____ personal distance, which has a close phase of one and a half to two and a half feet; it is at this distance that wives usually stand from their husbands in public. If another woman moves into this zone, the wife will most likely be disturbed. The far phase—two and a half to four feet—is the distance used to "keep someone at arm's length" and is the most common spacing used by people in conversation. _____ social distance, which is employed during business transactions or exchanges with a clerk or repairman. People who work together tend to use close social distance, four to seven feet. The far phase of the third zone—seven to twelve feet—is where people stand when someone says, "Stand back so I can look at you." This distance lends a formal tone to business or social discourse. _____ public distance, which is used by teachers in classrooms or speakers at public gatherings. At its farthest phase—twenty-five feet and beyond—it is used for important public figures.[1]

EXERCISE 3-4
Analyzing an Enumerative Paragraph

Directions: Fill in the following chart, which is based on the paragraph you read in Exercise 3-3.

Topic Sentence:

[1]Adapted from Edward T. Hall and Mildred Reed Hall, "The Sounds of Silence," *Playboy,* June 1971, pp. 138–140, 148, 204, 206.

ZONE	PHASES, DISTANCES	USES
1. Intimate distance	The near phase (physical contact to six inches)	
	The far phase (six to eighteen inches)	
2.		
3.		
4.		

ASCENDING VS. DESCENDING ORDER

Up to this point, the paragraphs in this unit have been structured so that all their parts are *of equal importance*. Thus, in the sample paragraph on library materials (p. 40), no kind of library material is presented as being more important than any other kind; the paragraph represents, as we have already said, a simple, straightforward list.

The same thing can be said of the paragraph which talks about the writer's two main reasons for attending Bingston University (page 10). If you remember, there was nothing in the paragraph to suggest that one reason was considered any more important than the other. This paragraph, too, represents a simple list:

MY TWO MAIN REASONS FOR ATTENDING BINGSTON UNIVERSITY

1. Reasonable tuition; the deferred payment plan
   (financial reasons)
2. Fine teachers; practical work experience
   (academic reasons)

Sometimes, however, a writer wishes to indicate that one of the items in a list should receive special attention. In other words, the writer feels that one item is *more important, more interesting, more influential, stronger, bigger,* or *more basic* than the other items on the list. There are two ways in which an item can be singled out in a written paragraph: *ascending* and *descending* order.

ASCENDING ORDER

In ascending order, we list the minor points first, *saving the most important for last.* This keeps the reader interested, since the paragraph has a kind of "dramatic structure" to it; it builds up to or ascends to a climax. In a list using numerals, this can easily be indicated by drawing a circle or an arrow, by underlining, or by all three at the same time—anything to *catch the reader's eye.* In a written paragraph, however, we cannot do this. We indicate ascending order by means of a special group of listing signals:

GROUP 3 (ASCENDING ORDER)

But by far the	[MOST ESSENTIAL MOST IMPORTANT PRIMARY LARGEST (ETC.)]	[kind reason (etc.)]	is _____.
Finally—AND MOST IMPORTANTLY—there is _____.			

Let us illustrate the difference between a *list* in ascending order and a *paragraph* in ascending order. We will take the subject of Bingston University, since we are already familiar with the information. Let us say this time that there are four reasons why the writer wants to attend Bingston University: its reasonable tuition, its deferred payment plan, its work/study program, and its fine teachers. We will also assume that the *work/study program* is what really attracts the writer to Bingston. A list which says all this might look something like the following:

MY REASONS FOR CHOOSING BINGSTON

1. Its reasonable tuition
2. Its deferred payment plan
3. Its fine teachers
4. Its work/study program

In paragraph form, the same information might look like this:

There were several reasons why I decided to attend Bingston University. First of all, the tuition was reasonable. Second, the university had a deferred payment plan; this represented a great convenience to my parents. Another reason was the fact that Bingston hires only the finest of teachers to teach in its graduate program. *My chief reason,* however, was Bingston's mandatory work/study program in agriculture, my chosen field: the university requires all agriculture students to gain practical experience by working on farms in the area while they are still going to school; I knew that this would provide invaluable experience and prepare me to better use the skills I had learned in the classroom.

DESCENDING ORDER

In *descending order,* the writer lists the most important point *first,* then goes on to speak of the other points. The writer usually thinks that the other points are important, too; he simply wishes to mention the most important one first. Thus, descending order is essentially the inverse of ascending order. Descending order, too, has its special *listing signals:*

GROUP 4 (DESCENDING ORDER)

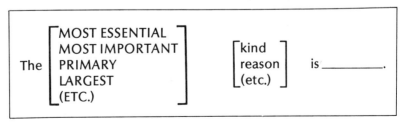

The list of the writer's reasons for attending Bingston University, rewritten in *descending order,* would look like this:

MY REASONS FOR CHOOSING BINGSTON

① Its work/study program
2. Its fine teachers
3. Its deferred payment plan
4. Its reasonable tuition

In paragraph form, the information might look like this:

There were several reasons why I decided to attend Bingston University. My <u>chief</u> reason for choosing that university was its wonderful work/study program in agriculture, my chosen field. The university requires all its agriculture students to gain practical experience by working on farms in the area while they are still going to school; I knew that this would provide invaluable experience and prepare me to better use the skills I had learned in the classroom. Second, Bingston hires only the finest teachers to teach in its graduate program. Then, too, there was Bingston's deferred payment plan; this represented a great convenience to my parents. A final reason was the reasonable tuition.

NOW ASK YOURSELF

1. What is "enumeration by *equal* order"?_____

    _____

2. How do *ascending* and *descending* order differ? _____

    _____

3. How are simple enumerative lists different from formal enumerative

    paragraphs? _____

    _____

    _____

    _____

EQUAL ORDER	ASCENDING ORDER	DESCENDING ORDER

Topic Sentence

(The writer feels that all the items are EQUALLY IMPORTANT)

Topic Sentence

MOST IMPORTANT

(The writer feels that one item is more important, essential, etc., than the others. He places it LAST.)

Topic Sentence

MOST IMPORTANT

(The writer feels that one item is more important, essential, etc., than the others. He places it FIRST.)

EXERCISE 3-5
Analyzing Enumerative Paragraphs
(Simple List Form)

Directions: After reading each of the following paragraphs carefully, determine which order it illustrates (equal, ascending, or descending). Then indicate all *enumerators* and *listing signals* which the author has used to structure the paragraph. Finally, construct a *simple list* which represents the structure of the paragraph. The first has been done as an example.

1.　　Of the ten largest retailing companies in the United States, three are involved in mail-order sales. The top mail-order company is Sears, Roebuck and Co., with yearly sales of over $17 million and assets of almost $15 million. Next comes J.C. Penney, whose yearly sales total more than $9 million and whose assets are approximately $4 million. The smallest mail-order company in the top-ten grouping is Montgomery Ward, which has over $4 million in yearly sales and assets of nearly $3 million.

Type of order used: ___ descending order _____

Enumerator(s): ___ company _____

Listing signals: ___ the top; next; the smallest _____

50

Paragraph Structure (simple list form)

MAIL-ORDER COMPANIES WHICH FIGURE IN THE TOP-TEN LIST:

⟶ ①. Sears, Roebuck and Co. _____

2. J. C. Penney _____

3. Montgomery Ward _____

_____

_____

_____

_____

_____

_____

2.   Astronomers use three basic types of telescopes to explore the
vastness of space. The *refractor* telescope uses two lenses—one to
collect light from a distant object and bring it into focus, and another
in the eyepiece to magnify the image. Second, there is the *reflector*
telescope, which makes use of a concave mirror instead of a lens to
reflect light rays to the upper end of the telescope. Last, and perhaps most important in terms of studying phenomena outside the
earth's atmosphere, is the *radio* telescope, which gathers waves
with a wire antenna serving as a parabolic reflecting surface. The
discovery of mysterious quasars and pulsars was made possible by
this kind of telescope.

Type or order used: _____

Enumerator(s): _____

Listing signals: _____

Paragraph Structure (Simple List Form)

_____

_____

_____

_____

_____

_____

_____

_____

_____

_____

_____

3.   Congested airways, as determined by the number of passengers served each year, are becoming as serious a problem in major U.S. cities as congested highway traffic. During 1977, 13.2 million passengers boarded, deplaned, or transferred through Washington, D.C.'s National Airport. San Francisco's International served 20.2 million people during the same period. The nation's busiest airport, however, was Chicago's O'Hare Field, where over 44 million passengers were served.

Type of order used: _____

Enumerator(s): _____

Listing signals: _____

Paragraph Structure (Simple List Form)

_____

_____

_____

_____

_____

_____

_____

_____

_____

_____

_____

_____

4.   Because the earth turns on its axis at the same time as it is moving around the sun, there are two ways to determine the period of time which constitutes a day. It is possible to define a day as the interval of time between the highest point of the sun in the sky on two successive days. This determination, "mean solar time," produces the twenty-four-hour day when it is averaged out over the year. It is equally possible, however, to define a day as that period of time between the points when the vernal equinox is directly overhead. This method of measuring is called "sidereal time" and is almost four minutes shorter per day than solar mean time.

Type of order used: _____

Enumerator(s): _____

Listing signals: _____

Paragraph Structure (Simple List Form)

_____

_____

_____

_____

_____

_____

_____

_____

_____

_____

*5.   Bioethicists, a new breed of scientist-philosophers, concern themselves with pressing problems which have arisen as a result of technological advances in modern medicine. One consideration is the recent development of techniques which enable doctors to perform test-tube cross-fertilization, producing the famous "test-tube babies." Recombinant DNA, or genetic engineering, is another medical achievement which is accompanied by dubious moral implications. Artificial organ implantation (heart, kidneys, eyes) generates questions of who should be chosen as recipient of these life-sustaining gifts and how these choices should be made. On the opposite end of the spectrum, machines which are capable of prolonging life indefinitely, even though the patient may never regain consciousness, bring up the problem of establishing a precise definition of what "death" is.

Type of order used:_____

Enumerator(s):_____

Listing signals:_____

Paragraph Structure (Simple List Form)

_____

_____

_____

_____

_____

_____

_____

_____

_____

*6.   Various answers have been proposed to the gnawing question which reflects one of man's deepest needs: How is it possible to overcome the awareness of human separation, the overpowering feeling of aloneness? One way of achieving this aim lies in the so-called orgiastic states, such as the hypnosis-producing rituals of "primitive" tribes, or alcoholism and drug addiction in our own society. Another, and far more frequent, solution is a union with others based on conformity—in dress, customs, ideas, and even daily routine. A third way of attaining union lies in creative activity: the artist unites himself with his material, which represents the world outside himself. But the problem with this union, as with the first two mentioned, is that none of them is personal, and all are transitory. By far the only permanent answer to this great problem of human existence lies in the achievement of _interpersonal_ union, of fusion with another person. In other words, it lies only in _love._ Mature love is the ultimate force which breaks the walls separating man from his fellow men, the force which unites him with others, thus allowing him to overcome his sense of isolation. In love, the paradox occurs that two human beings remain two, yet become one.[2]

[2]Adapted from Erich Fromm, _The Art of Loving_ (New York: Harper & Row, Publishers, Inc., 1956), pp. 7–17.

Type of order used: _____

Enumerator(s): _____

Listing signals: _____

Paragraph Structure (Simple List Form)

_____

_____

_____

_____

_____

_____

_____

_____

_____

_____

EXERCISE 3-6
Practicing Ascending, Descending,
and Equal Order

Directions: Using the information given, write three five-sentence paragraphs: the first in *equal* order, the second in *ascending* order, and the third in *descending* order. Be sure to write complete sentences.

PROBLEMS FACING OLD PEOPLE IN THE UNITED STATES

1. Poverty
2. Sickness
3. Transportation
4. Loneliness

Equal Order

_____

_____

_____

_____

_____

Ascending Order

_____

_____

_____

_____

_____

Descending Order

_____

_____

_____

_____

_____

Directions: Write an enumerative paragraph based on the following chart. Use *descending order*. Decide what your basis of enumeration will be (number of members or age).

FIVE MAJOR RELIGIONS

	Number of Members	Basis of Belief	Dates of Origin	Geographic Distribution
Judaism	14,353,790	Descent from Israel; *The Torah;* tradition	The exodus of Moses from Egypt (1220 B.C.)	Worldwide
Christianity	954,766,700	The teachings of Jesus Christ: *The New Testament*	c. A.D. 33 (Jesus Christ)	Worldwide
Islam	538,213,900	The teachings of Mohammed in *The Koran*	A.D. 570–632 (Mohammed)	Morocco to Indonesia; a branch in the United States
Hinduism	524,273,050	*The Vedas* (four books); no common creed	1000 B.C. (?)	India and eastern countries
Buddhism	249,877,300	The teachings of Buddha in *The Eightfold Way*	563–483 B.C. (Buddha)	The east; spreading to Europe and the United States

_____

_____

_____

_____

_____

EXERCISE 3-8
Paragraph Writing: Enumeration

Directions: Write an enumerative paragraph in which you tell of *the qualities which a good wife or husband should have.* Use good examples, details, etc., in developing the paragraph. Use *ascending order.*

_____

_____

_____

_____

_____

Optional Writing Assignments (Enumeration)

1. The things (at least three) that I have learned about Americans since I came to the United States.
2. My favorite kinds of movies.
3. The types of undergraduate degrees offered at a particular school. (You may have to use a university catalog to research this topic.)

4

SPECIAL TYPES
OF ENUMERATION

Process and Chronology

In this chapter we will deal with two specialized types of enumerative paragraphs: the *process* paragraph and the *chronological* (or narrative) paragraph. Since a process paragraph uses many of the listing signals you learned in the previous chapter, will will start with this type.

PROCESS

When supporting sentences are arranged in a step-by-step sequence which *tells how something is made or done,* this development is called *process.* Process development is, in fact, a kind of enumeration, but here we are usually dealing only with *steps* or *stages* (and not, for example, with kinds or types). If we wanted to give a more visual representation of process development, our diagram might look something like this:

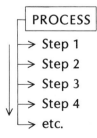

Model Paragraph

In his will, Alfred Nobel left specific instructions as to how the winners of the science awards he endowed are to be selected. First, each year the Swedish Academy of Sciences (physics and chemistry) and the Caroline Medical Institute (physiology and medicine) solicit nearly two thousand recommendations from past laureates, university professors, and other experts from all over the world. The second step is the review of recommendations received and the selections of preliminary candidates by special committees within the two Swedish institutions. The committee members are specifically instructed that those chosen "shall have conferred the greatest benefit on mankind," and that no consideration be given to the candidates' nationalities. Next, after lengthy investigation and discussion, the final choices are made for each discipline. Finally, telegrams informing them of their awards are sent to the new Nobel laureates about one month prior to the award ceremony.

▶ *NOW ASK YOURSELF*

1. What are the key words in the topic sentence? (Is there anything in the topic sentence which suggests that the paragraph will be explaining a

   process?) _____

   _____

2. Can you find any enumerative *listing signals?* _____

   _____

3. Have any *enumerators* been used (i.e., words like *steps* or *stages*)?

   _____

4. Between the first step (soliticing requests for recommendations) and the last step (informing the new laureates), how many steps can you find?

   _____

   _____

   _____

   _____

EXERCISE 4-1
Analyzing a Process Paragraph (List Form)

Directions: Show the organization of the model paragraph by filling in the following list. You do not have to write complete sentences.

How _____

1. _____

2. _____

3. _____

4. _____

5. _____

6. _____

EXERCISE 4-2
Analyzing a Process Paragraph (Chart Form)

Directions: Now you are ready to expand the above list by filling in a chart. Indicate, in *note form,* any kinds of supportive information which you have found in the paragraph:

Examples

Details

Anecdotes

Facts and statistics

Topic Sentence: ___ In his will, _____

_____

_____

STEP	SUPPORTIVE MATERIAL (Examples, Details, Etc.)
1. Requests for recommendations	Swedish Academy of Sciences (physics, chemistry) Caroline Medical Institute (physiology, medicine) Two thousand requests from past laureates, university professors, and experts
2.	
3.	
4.	
5.	
6.	

ENUMERATORS

Process paragraphs, like other kinds of enumerative paragraphs, often use enumerators. The difference is that, whereas enumerative paragraphs use many different enumerators (*types, kinds, groups,* etc.), process paragraphs most commonly use only *three*:

Step

Stage

Phase

1. In the paragraph on finding a suitable apartment (p. 13), do you notice any of these enumerators? _____

2. In the paragraph on changing a flat tire (p. 18), do you notice any of these enumerators? _____

3. What about the model paragraph which you have just read (Nobel Prize)? _____

LISTING SIGNALS

Process paragraphs often use listing signals. *Group 1* listing signals from the previous chapter (p. 42) can be used, but the structures which follow them are usually different:

Group 1 (PROCESS)

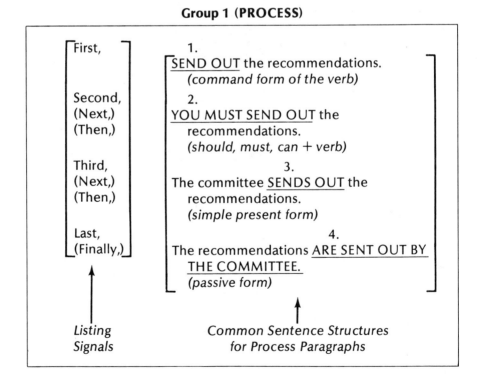

NOW ASK YOURSELF

Which of the above structures do the following sentences represent—command form, modal auxiliaries, simple present, or passive?

(From "Changing a Flat Tire," p. 18)

1. The jack should be correctly placed.   _____

2. . . . carefully loosen the nuts. . . .   _____

3. Remove the tire and put the spare tire   _____
   in place.

(From "Finding a Suitable Apartment," p. 13)

4. . . . you must follow a very systematic   _____
   approach.

5. First, you must decide which neighbor-   _____
   hood. . . .

6. . . . you should check under. . . .   _____

7. Otherwise, check under. . . .   _____

(From "Nobel Prize Winners," p. 63)

8. . . . the Swedish Academy of Sciences . . .   _____
   and the Caroline Medical Institute . . .
   solicit nearly two thousand requests for
   recommendations. . . .

9. The committee members are specifically   _____
   instructed that. . . .

10. . . . the final choices are made. . . .   _____

Group 2 listing signals from the previous chapter (p. 43) can also be used to develop process paragraphs:

Group 2 (PROCESS)

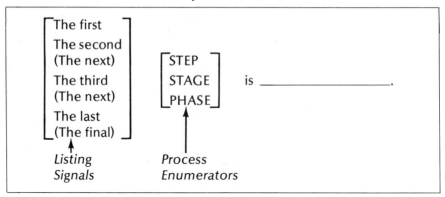

 NOW ASK YOURSELF

Examine the three paragraphs ("Finding a Suitable Apartment," "Changing a Flat Tire," and "Nobel Prize Winners") once again, this time looking for Group 2 listing signals + enumerators. Do you find any?

1. "Finding a Suitable Apartment" (p. 13)_____

   _____

2. "Changing a Flat Tire" (p. 18)_____

   _____

3. "Nobel Prize Winners" (p. 63)_____

   _____

EXERCISE 4-3
Analyzing Process Paragraphs (List Form)

Directions: Construct *simple lists* for "Finding a Suitable Apartment" (p. 13) and "Changing a Flat Tire" (p. 18). Be sure to *number* each item to show its order in the process.

FINDING A SUITABLE APARTMENT	CHANGING A FLAT TIRE
_____	_____
_____	_____
_____	_____
_____	_____
_____	_____
_____	_____
_____	_____
_____	_____

TIME CLUES, REPETITION, AND PRONOUN REFERENCE

In addition to sequence signals, there are other indicators which a writer can use to develop a process paragraph. They are

1. *Time clues*, which include choice of verb and tense
2. *Repetition*, which provides links between your sentences, thus helping the reader following your train of thought
3. *Pronoun reference*, which provides still another kind of link between your sentences

TIME CLUES

Now study the following model paragraph. It is given here to illustrate *time clues*. It will be given again, several pages later, to illustrate repetition and pronoun reference.

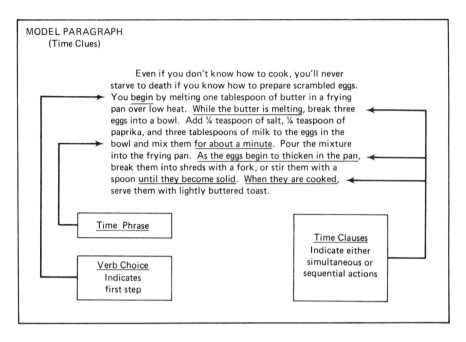

MODEL PARAGRAPH
(Time Clues)

Even if you don't know how to cook, you'll never starve to death if you know how to prepare scrambled eggs. You begin by melting one tablespoon of butter in a frying pan over low heat. While the butter is melting, break three eggs into a bowl. Add ¼ teaspoon of salt, ¼ teaspoon of paprika, and three tablespoons of milk to the eggs in the bowl and mix them for about a minute. Pour the mixture into the frying pan. As the eggs begin to thicken in the pan, break them into shreds with a fork, or stir them with a spoon until they become solid. When they are cooked, serve them with lightly buttered toast.

Time Phrase

Verb Choice
Indicates
first step

Time Clauses
Indicate either
simultaneous or
sequential actions

Verb Choice. In the model paragraph, the choice of the verb *begin* indicates the first step or stage. Another appropriate verb choice would be *start*. There are other verbs which can be used to indicate the various parts of a process. Some of them are shown below:

STEP (STAGE)	VERBS
First ——————➤	BEGIN START
Intermediate ——➤	CONTINUE BECOME REMAIN DEVELOP
Final ——————➤	END FINISH CULMINATE

Time Clauses. Time clauses and phrases also help in showing the continuity of development in a process. In the model paragraph, the time clauses explain the time relationship between events just as clearly as sequence signals do:

> *While* the butter is melting
>
> *As* the eggs begin to thicken in the pan
>
> *When* they are cooked

The most common time words used to introduce time clauses are *before, after, when, while, as,* and *until*. Study the following box:

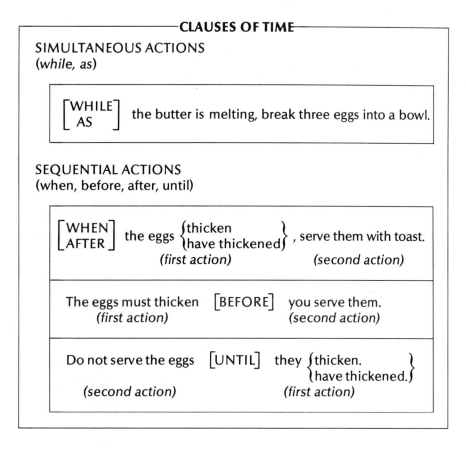

CLAUSES OF TIME

SIMULTANEOUS ACTIONS
(*while, as*)

[WHILE / AS] the butter is melting, break three eggs into a bowl.

SEQUENTIAL ACTIONS
(when, before, after, until)

[WHEN / AFTER] the eggs {thicken / have thickened}, serve them with toast.
      (first action)   *(second action)*

The eggs must thicken [BEFORE] you serve them.
    (first action)   *(second action)*

Do not serve the eggs [UNTIL] they {thicken. / have thickened.}
    (second action)   *(first action)*

Participial Phrases Sometimes time clauses may be reduced to *participial phrases*. Study the following box; note that the structure of the clauses is not the same as the structure of the (participial) time phrases:

PARTICIPIAL PHRASES

SIMULTANEOUS ACTIONS
(while)

Clause: While you are melting the butter, break three eggs
          into a bowl.

——►Phrase: | While melting the butter, ... |

SEQUENTIAL ACTIONS
(when, after, before)

Clause: ⎡When⎤ you have beaten the eggs, pour them into
          ⎣After ⎦   the pan.

——►Phrase: | Having beaten the eggs, ...
             | After having beaten the eggs, ... |

Clause: You must beat the eggs before you pour them into
                                                  the pan.

——►Phrase: | . . . before pouring them into the pan. |

Sentence Connectors of Time   Sometimes, instead of making one of the sentences into a time clause, we can join the two sentences by a sentence connector of time. This can be either a word or a phrase. Study the following box. Notice the use of the *semicolon.* A semicolon is used to punctuate the two sentences which are being joined by the sentence connectors in each of the examples. That is, the semicolon combines two grammatically distinct sentences into one. This is done because of the *strong meaning link* between them, expressed by the sentence connectors. The semicolon is commonly used to punctuate sentences when sentence connectors are used:

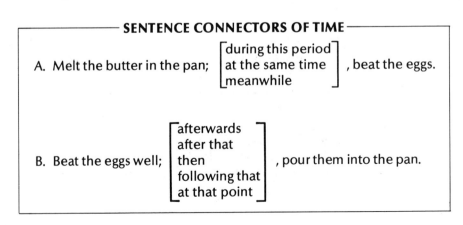

SENTENCE CONNECTORS OF TIME

A. Melt the butter in the pan;   ⎡during this period⎤
                                  ⎢at the same time ⎢ , beat the eggs.
                                  ⎣meanwhile   ⎦

B. Beat the eggs well;   ⎡afterwards   ⎤
                         ⎢after that   ⎢
                         ⎢then   ⎢ , pour them into the pan.
                         ⎢following that ⎢
                         ⎣at that point ⎦

72

 *NOW ASK YOURSELF*

Can the above two sentences be rewritten using a period in place of the semicolon? If so, rewrite them:

_____

_____

EXERCISE 4-4
Identifying Time Clues

Directions: Below you will find two process paragraphs from Unit One. Try to find the following items in each of the paragraphs, labeling each item clearly:

1. Verb choice which indicates process
2. Time clause
3. Participial phrase of time
4. Sentence connector of time

In order to find a suitable apartment, you must follow a very systematic approach. First, you must decide which neighborhood would be most convenient for you. Then you must determine how much rent your budget will allow. Utility bills for apartments average between fifty and seventy dollars per month. Your next step is to check the classified ads in the newspapers. Be sure to check these ads regularly, since new listings appear each day. After you have telephoned the apartments which seem likely choices, you must begin your long journey to inspect each one of them.

Changing a flat tire is really not a very complicated process. When you have removed the hubcap from the wheel which has the flat, the jack should be correctly placed so as to be able to lift the car off the ground. Jack up the car high enough for the tire to clear the ground; at that point, carefully loosen the nuts that hold the tire and rim in place by using your lug wrench. Proceed by removing the flat tire and putting the spare tire in its place. Now you are ready to put the nuts back on the wheel and tighten them well with the lug wrench. All that remains is to replace the hubcap.

EXERCISE 4-5
Paraphrasing Sentences Using Time Clues

Directions: The following sentences are based on the model paragraph dealing with the Nobel Prize. Rewrite each of the sentences in two different ways, using the words or phrases indicated. Refer to the charts as often as necessary. Pay attention to *punctuation.* In the case of participial phrases, make sure that the subject of the sentence is the same as the implied subject of the participial phrase.

1. The Swedish Academy of Science solicits recommendations in the fields of physics and chemistry; the Caroline Medical Institute solicits recommendations in the fields of physiology and medicine.

   (while) While the Swedish Academy of Science solicits recommendations in the fields of physics and chemistry, the Caroline Medical Institute solicits recommendations in the fields of physiology and medicine.

   (at the same time) The Swedish Academy of Science _____

   _____

   _____

2. Requests are sent out; recommendations are received from past laureates, university professors, and experts all over the world.

   (after) _____

   _____

   (after that) _____

   _____

3. The committees receive all recommendations; they begin reviewing them.

   (when) _____

   _____

(PARTICIPIAL PHRASE) ___Having_____

_____

4. The committee members review the recommendations; they are instructed that no consideration be given to the candidates' nationalities.

   (as) _____

   _____

   (at the same time) _____

   _____

5. The committee members review the recommendations; preliminary
   choices are made.

   (PARTICIPIAL PHRASE) ___Having_____

   _____

   (before) _____

   _____

6. The committees conduct lengthy investigations and have long discus-
   sions; the final choices are made.

   (PARTICIPIAL PHRASE) ___After having_____

   _____

   (until) _____

   _____

7. The final choices are made; telegrams are sent to the new Nobel
   laureates.

   (PARTICIPIAL PHRASE) ___After making_____

   _____

   (then) _____

   _____

(until) _____

_____

(VERB CHOICE—final step) _____

_____

REPETITION AND PRONOUN REFERENCE

MODEL PARAGRAPH

Even if you don't know how to cook, you'll never starve to death if you know how to prepare scrambled eggs. You begin by melting one tablespoon of butter in a frying pan over low heat. While the butter is melting, break three eggs into a bowl. Add ¼ teaspoon of salt, ¼ teaspoon of paprika, and three tablespoons of milk to the eggs in the bowl and mix them for about a minute. Pour the mixture into the frying pan. As the eggs begin to thicken in the pan, break them into shreds with a fork, or stir them with a spoon until they become solid. When they are cooked, serve them with lightly buttered toast.

Notice that words are often repeated to add continuity to a paragraph. They are repeated either in their *original* form or in *pronoun* form. In the model paragraph above, take note of the following:

> The words *eggs*, *bowl*, and *mix* (as well as its word form *mixture*)
>
> The different pronouns which mean "eggs"

All of these things, in addition to sequence signals, add a sense of continuity and *cohesiveness* to a paragraph's development, and they are particularly important in a process paragraph. Pay particular attention to this sort of clue when you write.

EXERCISE 4-6
Identifying Pronoun and Repetition Clues

Directions: What repeated words and pronoun forms do you find in the following paragraphs? Circle them, draw lines to connect them, and label them clearly in the margins.

In order to find a suitable apartment, you must follow a very systematic approach. First, you must decide which neighborhood would be most convenient for you. Then you must determine how much rent your budget will allow. Utility bills for apartments average between fifty and seventy dollars per month. Your next step is to check the classified ads in the newspapers. Be sure to check these ads regularly, since new listings appear each day. After you have telephoned the apartments which seem likely choices, you must begin your long journey to inspect each one of them.

Changing a flat tire is really not a very complicated process. When you have removed the hubcap from the wheel which has the flat, the jack should be correctly placed so as to be able to lift the car off the ground. Jack up the car high enough for the tire to clear the ground; at that point, carefully loosen the nuts that hold the tire and rim in place by using your lug wrench. Proceed by removing the flat tire and putting the spare tire in its place. Now you are ready to put the nuts back on the wheel and tighten them well with the lug wrench. All that remains is to replace the hubcap.

The telephone, like the computer, acts on information presented to it and produces a result. The input is the actual dialing of the number. The switching system which locates the number can be considered the processing phase. Finally, the telephone rings on the other end of the line, indicating that the call has been completed; this constitutes the output.

EXERCISE 4-7
Unscrambling a Process Paragraph

Directions: The sentences below constitute a paragraph on the scientific method. However, the sentences have been given a *disordered sequence*—that is, they have been *scrambled.* You should place them in their correct order and, if your teacher wishes, copy the reconstructed paragraph. When you have finished, answer the questions which follow.

    a. Following this method, the researcher first observes some aspects of nature and then poses a specific question about what he has observed.

    b. Experiments based on this hypothesis are designed and conducted to test each contingency.

    c. In order to answer this question, pertinent data are collected.

    d. After thorough experimentation, the researcher validates, modifies, or rejects his original hypothesis.

e. Originating from the branch of philosophy called epistemology, what we now know as the scientific method provides guidelines for the systematic acquisition of knowledge.

f. On the basis of these data, a hypothesis is proposed to explain them.

_____

_____

_____

_____

_____

_____

_____

_____

_____

_____

_____

_____

_____

_____

_____

_____

_____

_____

_____

_____

_____

_____

Questions

1. Which words are repeated in the paragraph? _____

    _____

2. Are process enumerators used (steps, stages, etc.)? _____

3. Are any *listing signals* used (First, Second, Next, Then, etc.)? _____

    _____

4. Are there any *time clauses* (when, while, after, before, until)? _____

    _____

5. Are there any *participial time phrases* (-ing form)? _____

6. Are there any sentence connectors of time (after that, afterwards,

    meanwhile)? _____

    _____

7. What does each of the five pronouns in the passage refer to:

    this method: _____

    this question: _____

    these data: _____

    them: _____

    this hypothesis: _____

Go back to the rewritten paragraph and draw arrows from each of these
pronouns to the word or phrase it represents.

*EXERCISE 4-8
Unscrambling a Process Paragraph

Directions: Unscramble the following sentences and, if your teacher wishes, copy them in their correct order in the spaces given. Then answer the questions which follow.

    a. He has usually learned the language and is thus able to laugh at himself.

    b. Having passed through these stages of culture shock, he may even eventually return home with regret at having lost his "adopted home."

    c. The process of reacting and adjusting to a new society, sometimes termed culture shock, has four distinct stages.

    d. A hostile attitude is typical of the second stage, which develops at that point when the individual has to seriously cope with the day-to-day problems of housing, shopping, transportation, etc.

    e. Final adjustment to a new culture occurs when the visitor is able to function without anxiety and to accept what he finds for what it is—another way of doing things.

    f. During this initial encounter, every aspect of the new society seems fascinating and new.

    g. The first period, or "honeymoon stage," may last as long as several months.

    h. The visitor develops a sense of humor about his problems as he enters the third stage.

    i. The visitor usually begins his stay in a hotel and meets sympathetic and gracious nationals.

    j. He soon finds that most people in the new society are indifferent to these problems, so he seeks out his fellow countrymen to support him in his criticism of the host country.

_____

_____

_____

_____

_____

_____

_____

_____

_____

_____

Questions

1. Are words *repeated* in the passage? _____

2. Are process *enumerators* used (step, stage, etc.)? _____

3. Are any *listing signals* used (first, second, third, etc.)? _____

   _____

4. Are there any *time clauses* (when, while, before, after, as, until)? _____

   _____

5. Are there any *participial phrases of time* (-ing form)? _____

   _____

6. Are there any *sentence connectors of time* (after that, afterwards, meanwhile)? _____

7. Circle all *pronouns* which refer back to something previously mentioned in the passage. Draw an arrow back to the thing mentioned. (This is a good way to check the accuracy of your unscrambling.)

EXERCISE 4-9
Paragraph Writing:
Process Information Transfer

Directions: After studying the following series of drawings, write a process paragraph based on them. Use the topic sentence which has been provided. Then construct a simple list which shows the steps in the process.

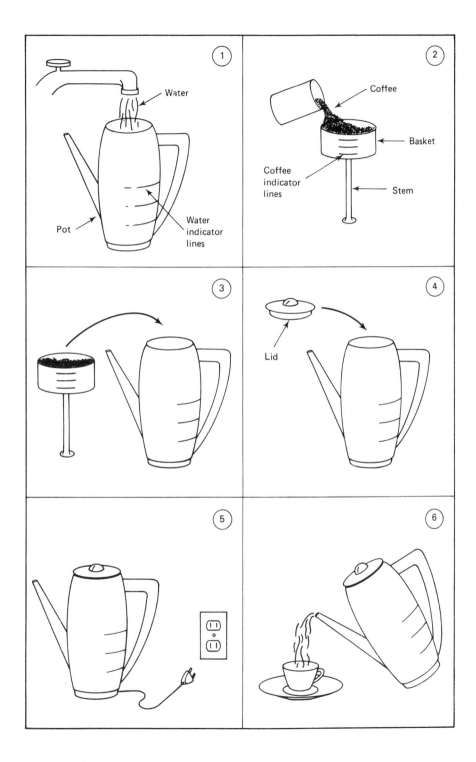

Making a pot of coffee is quite a simple matter if you have an electric percolator. _____

_____

_____

_____

_____

_____

_____

_____

_____

_____

_____

_____

_____

_____

_____

Paragraph Structure (Simple List Form)

EXERCISE 4-10
Paragraph Writing: Process

Directions: Explain, in a step-by-step fashion, the procedures that one must go through in applying to a school in the United States or in your own country.

_____

_____

_____

_____

_____

_____

_____

_____

_____

_____

_____

_____

_____

_____

_____

_____

_____

_____

_____

_____

_____

_____

_____

CHRONOLOGICAL ORDER

When the order in which things happen, or a *time sequence,* is used to develop a paragraph, this is called *chronological order.* Like process, this is a special form of enumeration, since it is really a *list of events.*

Model Paragraph

Although the U. S. Air Force was not officially created until after the Second World War, it had existed under other names since the beginning of the century. The Army Air Forces were started on August 1,

1907, as a part of the Aeronautical Division of the U.S. Signal Corps, and it was more than one year later that this small division carried out its first mission in its own airplane. When the United States entered World War I in 1917, the Aviation Service, as it was then called, had only thirty-five pilots. On December 7, 1941, the renamed Army Air Forces had only three thousand of their ten thousand planes ready for combat. Finally, in 1947, the U. S. Air Force was established as a separate branch of the military.

ANALYSIS ("TIME LINE")

Topic Sentence: Although the U.S. Air Force was not officially created until after the Second World War, it had existed under other names since the beginning of the century.

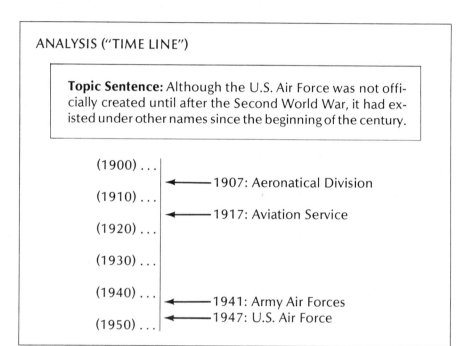

(1900) . . .

(1910) . . . ◄————1907: Aeronatical Division

◄————1917: Aviation Service

(1920) . . .

(1930) . . .

(1940) . . . ◄————1941: Army Air Forces

◄————1947: U.S. Air Force

(1950) . . .

NOW ASK YOURSELF

1. Why do we classify chronological order as enumeration? _____

_____

2. What are the key words in the topic sentence of the model paragraph?

_____

3. What four main examples are given? _____

_____

4. What statistics have been used? _____

_____

5. Do you notice any enumerators and listing signals? _____

_____

Any time clauses? (Underline them in the paragraph.)

6. Make a simple list which demonstrates the structure of the model paragraph. Be sure to give your list a title.

LISTING SIGNALS

Enumerators are rarely used in chronological order. We might occasionally write "the next *thing*" or "the next *event*," but the reader does not usually need this kind of signal to understand what is being talked about.

However, we do often use *Group 1* Process Listing Signals. Refer back to page 66 at this point to refresh your memory.

▶ *NOW ASK YOURSELF*

Comparing the forms of the *verbs* in the box on page 66 with the forms of the verbs in the model paragraph which you have just read, what is one way in which *process* differs from *narrative chronological order?*

_____

_____

_____

_____

_____

_____

TIME CLUES

Time clues of all kinds are, of course, *very* often used in chronology. Once again, however, as with listing signals, the forms of the verbs are not generally present forms, as they were in process, but rather *past* forms. In addition, prepositional phrases of time often appear:

```
┌─── PREPOSITIONAL PHRASES OF TIME ───┐
  IN 1956
  IN January, February, etc.
  IN the afternoon, the morning, the evening
  AT 9:00
  AT noon, midnight, night
  ON Monday, Tuesday, etc.
  ON July 6
  ON July 6, 1955
└─────────────────────────────────────┘
```

▶ *NOW ASK YOURSELF*

Which prepositions of time are used with the following:

1. Days of the week? _____

2. Months of the year? _____

3. An exact date? _____

4. Parts of the day? (two prepositions) _____

5. A specific year? _____

6. A particular hour of the day? _____

EXERCISE 4-11
Controlled Writing: Tense Shift

Directions: Rewrite the model process paragraph on page 63 ("Nobel Prize Winners"). This time, assume that the entire process occurred several months ago. In other words, describe it as though you were describing a real past event. The topic sentence has been given to you.

Earlier this year, preparations were made once again to pick the new

Nobel laureates. _____

_____

_____

EXERCISE 4-12
Unscrambling a Chronological Paragraph

Directions: Place the scrambled sentences below in their correct order; use the time line as your work space. Then, if your teacher wishes, copy the reconstructed paragraph on the lines which have been provided.

a. First, I had to go to the post office.

b. Half of the letters were addressed to American business concerns.

c. I got up at 6:30 A.M.

d. When I left the train station, I took my boss's car to the garage for repairs.

e. When I arrived at the office, my boss had several things for me to do.

f. I left the house at 7:45.

g. The other half were addressed to foreign companies.

h. After typing the letters, I had to run several errands.

i. Yesterday morning was quite hectic for me.

j. Then I had to pick up a train ticket for my boss's wife.

k. He asked me to type twenty letters for him.

l. By 1:00 P.M., I was exhausted, so I decided to have a long, leisurely lunch.

ANALYSIS (Time Line)

Topic Sentence:

(6:00 A.M.)....

(7:00 A.M.)....

(8:00 A.M.)....

(9:00 A.M.)....

(10:00 A.M.)....

(11:00 A.M.)....

(12:00 P.M.)....

(1:00 P.M.)....

*EXERCISE 4-13
Unscrambling a Chronological Paragraph

Directions: The sentences below constitute a paragraph about Abraham Lincoln (February 12, 1809–April 14, 1865), the sixteenth president of the United States. Unscramble them by placing them in their correct order; use the time line as your work space. Then, if your teacher wishes, copy the reconstructed paragraph on the lines which have been provided.

a. After having served only this one term in the U.S. Congress, he was defeated for reelection and returned to practice law in Springfield.

b. It was there that, having first tried his hand at a variety of occupations (storekeeper, postmaster, surveyor), he first became interested in politics.

c. He won the election, thus becoming the sixteenth president of the United States.

d. However, he was successful in his subsequent attempts, and served four two-year terms in the state legislature, from 1834 to 1842.

e. Shortly after passing the bar exam, he moved to Springfield, Illinois, to set up his own legal practice.

f. Lincoln's early political career did not foreshadow the success he was to have as president.

g. Indeed, he had almost entirely lost any hope of holding political office when, in 1854, the slavery question once again forced him into the political arena.

h. He was not successful the first time he ran for office in 1831.

i. During this same period he added the study of law to his legislative duties, finally being admitted to the Illinois bar in 1836.

j. In 1846, he was elected to the United States House of Representatives for two years.

k. Although he was defeated twice for election to the U. S. Congress, he finally managed, in 1860, to be nominated by the Republican Party as its candidate for president.

l. In his early twenties he moved to Illinois.

Topic Sentence:

(1810)....   ◄────── 1809: Lincoln's birth

(1820)....

(1830)....

(1840)....

(1850)....

(1860)....
                  ◄────── 1865: Lincoln's death
(1870)....

_____

_____

_____

_____

_____

_____

_____

_____

EXERCISE 4-14
Paragraph Writing:
Chronological Information Transfer

Directions: Below is a time line indicating some of the events in the life of John F. Kennedy. Using the topic sentence provided and the information on the time line, write a paragraph in which you use chronological development.

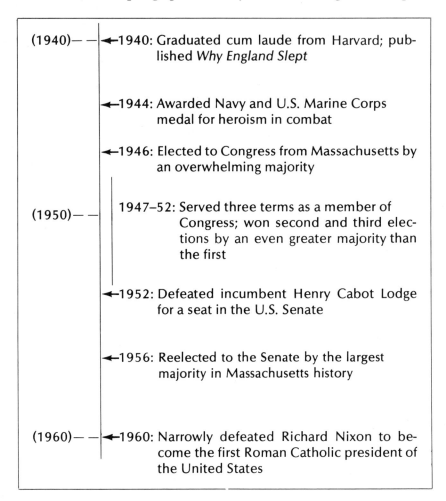

(1940)— —	◄—1940: Graduated cum laude from Harvard; published *Why England Slept*
	◄—1944: Awarded Navy and U.S. Marine Corps medal for heroism in combat
	◄—1946: Elected to Congress from Massachusetts by an overwhelming majority
(1950)— —	1947–52: Served three terms as a member of Congress; won second and third elections by an even greater majority than the first
	◄—1952: Defeated incumbent Henry Cabot Lodge for a seat in the U.S. Senate
	◄—1956: Reelected to the Senate by the largest majority in Massachusetts history
(1960)— —	◄—1960: Narrowly defeated Richard Nixon to become the first Roman Catholic president of the United States

Kennedy's early career foreshadowed the success he was to have as president. _____

_____

_____

EXERCISE 4-15
Paragraph Writing: Chronology

Directions: In a rather lengthy paragraph, give the chronology of the most interesting person in your family. You will not be able to include all of the details of this person's life, but you should try to list the events which make him (her) interesting.

An empty time line has been provided so that you can organize and note down the events you want to include. Spend some time doing this before you begin to write.

Topic Sentence: _____

_____

_____

_____

_____

_____

_____

_____

_____

_____

_____

_____

_____

_____

OPTIONAL WRITING ASSIGNMENTS
(Chronology and Process)

Chronology

1. Describe your first trip to the United States.
2. Write a chronology of your first few years at school.
3. Describe significant changes in your country's economy or culture within the last few years.

Process

1. Tell how to make your favorite dish.
2. Explain how to obtain a driver's license in the state where you are now living.
3. Describe the stages in forming a friendship.
4. Describe the steps involved in getting married in your country.

5

SUPPORTING TOPIC SENTENCES

Cause and Effect

In Unit Three, you learned how to divide a topic into its various types, characteristics, elements, parts, etc. Now we will concentrate on a type of paragraph development which is frequently very similar to enumeration: *cause and effect.* In other words, when you use a cause-effect method of development, this will often mean that you are supporting your topic sentence by listing or enumerating.

What you should remember, however, is that in a cause-effect development, there is always a *causal relationship* between the topic sentence and the supporting sentences, or even between major supporting sentences and minor ones. This means that your supporting sentences become a list of either *effects* (what a certain situation has lead to or has resulted in), or *causes* (reasons or explanations why something is the way it is, or why it happened the way it did):

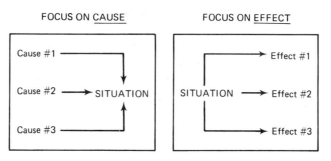

FOCUS ON <u>CAUSE</u>   FOCUS ON <u>EFFECT</u>

Cause #1 ———————┐   ┌—————————→ Effect #1

Cause #2 ——→ SITUATION   SITUATION ———→ Effect #2

Cause #3 ———————┘   └—————————→ Effect #3

We will look at each of these methods in the model paragraphs which follow. As you study each of them, look for: 1) supportive material such as examples, details, anecdotes, facts and statistics; 2) listing signals (enumeration); 3) ascending vs. descending order.

CAUSE-EFFECT DEVELOPMENT: FOCUS ON *EFFECT*

Model Paragraph

Many people are worried about what television has done to the generation of American children who have grown up watching it. For one thing, recent studies tend to show that TV stifles creative imagination. Some teachers feel that television has taken away the child's ability to form mental pictures in his own mind, resulting in children who cannot understand a simple story without visual illustrations. Secondly, too much TV too early tends to cause children to withdraw from real-life experiences. Thus, they grow up to be passive spectators who can only respond to action, but not initiate it. The third area for concern is the serious complaint frequently made by elementary school teachers that children exhibit a low tolerance for the frustrations of learning. Because they have been conditioned to see all problems resolved in 30 or 60 minutes on TV, they are quickly discouraged by any activity that promises less than instant gratification. But perhaps the most serious result is the impact of television violence on children, who have come to regard it as an everyday thing. Not only does this increase their tolerance of violent behavior in others, but most authorities now concede that under certain conditions, some children will imitate anti-social acts that they witness on television.[1]

Notice that the topic sentence introduces the idea of cause (i.e., television) and effect (i.e., what TV has done to children). The supporting sentences list or enumerate, and *explain,* the various bad effects of TV.

---

[1]Condensed from *Newsweek*, February 21, 1977. Copyright 1977 by Newsweek, Inc. All rights reserved. Reprinted by permission.

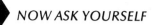

1. Have any enumerative listing signals been used? _____

   _____

2. Is the paragraph in *ascending, descending,* or *equal* order? How can

   you tell? _____

3. What kinds of supportive material can you find (examples, details, etc.)?

   _____

EXERCISE 5-1
Analyzing a Cause-Effect Paragraph
(Focus on Effect)

Directions: Fill in the chart below, which is based on the preceding model paragraph.

Topic Sentence: Many people are worried about what television has done to the generation of American children who have grown up watching it.

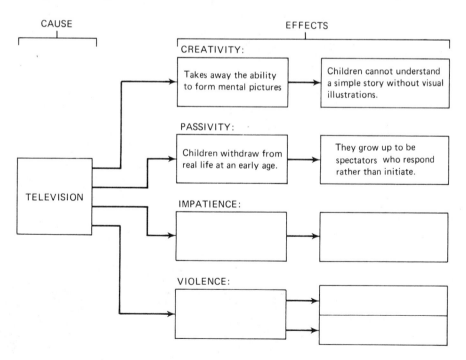

CAUSE-EFFECT DEVELOPMENT: STRUCTURAL SIGNALS

In addition to listing signals (First..., Second..., Finally,...; the first cause-effect..., the second cause-effect..., the final cause-effect...), certain other basic structures are commonly used in writing cause-effect paragraphs. There are two principle types:

I. SENTENCE CONNECTORS (i.e., words and phrases used to join *two complete grammatical sentences,* each with a subject and verb)

GROUP 1

Children watch too much television; *(cause)*	AS A RESULT, CONSEQUENTLY, THEREFORE, BECAUSE OF THIS, HENCE,	they lose creativity. *(effect)*

 NOW ASK YOURSELF

1. Which sentence is this kind of connector attached to—the one expressing *cause* or the one expressing *effect?*

    _____

2. Would it be possible to place the effect sentence first? _____

    (If so, do it:) _____

    _____

3. What are the names for the punctuation marks which have been used?

    (;) _____   (,) _____

4. Can the above sentence be rewritten without using a (;)?_____

    Using one of the connectors, try it: _____

    _____

104

GROUP 2

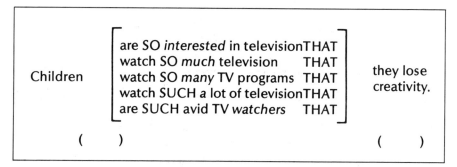

Children

are SO *interested* in televisionTHAT
watch SO *much* television   THAT
watch SO *many* TV programs THAT
watch SUCH *a* lot of televisionTHAT
are SUCH avid TV *watchers*   THAT

they lose creativity.

(   )   (   )

➤ *NOW ASK YOURSELF*

1. Which sentence expresses the cause? The effect? (Fill in the parentheses.)

2. How is the punctuation of Group 2 sentence connectors different from

   that of Group 1 connectors? _____

   When is *so . . . that* used? When is *such . . . that*? Can you formulate a rule?

   _____

   _____

   _____

GROUP 3

Children lose
creative ability
(   )

SINCE
BECAUSE
BECAUSE OF THE FACT THAT

they watch so much TV.
(   )

 NOW ASK YOURSELF

1. Which sentence expresses the cause? The effect? (Fill in the parentheses.)

2. Would it be possible to change the order of the sentences? If so, do it

(pay attention to punctuation): _____

_____

General Review of Sentence Connectors

A.   Which group of connectors place cause only *before* effect? _____

B.   Which groups place cause only *after* effect? _____

C.   Which groups place cause before *or* after effect? _____

II.   PREDICATE STRUCTURES (i.e., words and phrases which constitute the predicate of a *single* grammatical sentence; the choice of the verb indicates the cause-effect relationship)

GROUP 4

Watching too much television Too much television ( )	⌈ IS THE REASON FOR ⌉ IS RESPONSIBLE FOR LEADS TO CONTRIBUTES TO RESULTS IN ⌊ CAUSES ⌋	loss of creative ability. ( )

▶ *NOW ASK YOURSELF*

1.   Is the cause expressed in the subject of the sentence? _____

What about the object? _____ (Fill in the parentheses.)

2.   Can this order be reversed? If so, do it: _____

3.   Remembering that the verb *to cause* commonly takes another sentence structure in English, rewrite the sentence in the Group 4 chart in the

following way: "Too much television causes children _____

_____."

GROUP 5

Loss of creativity ( )	RESULTS FROM FOLLOWS FROM IS DUE TO IS A RESULT OF IS A CONSEQUENCE OF	watching too much television. too much television. ( )

 NOW ASK YOURSELF

1. Which part of the sentence expresses the *cause?* _____

2. Which part expresses the *effect?* _____

3. Can this order be reversed? If so, do it: _____

   _____

General Review of Verbal Structures

A. What seems to be the basic difference between Groups 4 and 5 and the

   previous three groups? _____

B. What seems to be the basic difference between Group 4 and Group 5

   (i.e., in the placement of *cause* and *effect*)? _____

   _____

EXERCISE 5-2
Paraphrasing Sentences of Cause-Effect

Directions: The following sentences are based on the model paragraph ("Harmful Effects of Television").

1. Rewrite each of the sentences in *two* different ways, using the words and phrases which have been indicated. (Refer back to the five charts as often as necessary if you need help.)

2. Pay particular attention to punctuation.

3. Indicate the *cause* and the *effect* in parentheses ( ) beneath each sentence, as in the example.

1. Loss of creative ability results from watching too much television.

    (therefore) <u>Children watch too much television; therefore, they lose</u>
    (cause)   (effect)
    <u>creative ability.</u>

    (so/such . . . that) <u>Children watch so much television that they lose</u>
    (cause)   (effect)
    <u>creative ability.</u>

2. Too much TV causes children to withdraw from real-life experiences.

    (is a consequence of) _____

    _____

    (because of the fact that) _____

    _____

3. Children develop a low tolerance for the frustrations of learning; hence,
    they are discouraged by any activity that does not give them instant
    gratification.

    (so/such . . . that) _____

    _____

    _____

    (cause [someone] to) _____

    _____

4. Another result of television violence is that children have come to regard
    it as an everyday thing.

    (because of this) _____

    _____

    (so/such . . . that) _____

    _____

5. Because of watching too much television, children expect every problem to be resolved in 30 or 60 minutes.

(result from) _____

_____

(because) _____

_____

6. Children cannot understand stories without visual illustrations because they cannot form pictures in their minds.

(consequently) _____

_____

(is due to) _____

_____

(Hint: Children's inability . . . their inability. . . .)

EXERCISE 5-3
Paragraph Writing:
Cause-Effect Information Transfer

Directions: After studying the chart, develop a paragraph. Use the topic sentence which has been provided.

VITAMIN	FUNCTION(S)	RESULT(S) OF DEFICIENCY
A	Normal vision; helps skin and mucous membranes resist infection	Night blindness; skin disease; degeneration of mucous membranes
B_1	Normal appetite and digestion; contributes to healthy nervous system	Beriberi; nervous disorders
B_2	Good skin and vision; helps cells use oxygen	Impaired growth

VITAMIN	FUNCTION(S)	RESULT(S) OF DEFICIENCY
B_6 and B_{12}	Normal hemoglobin; carries oxygen to tissues	Pernicious anemia; poor metabolism
C	Holds body cells together; aids in resisting infection	Scurvy
D	Healthy bones and teeth; aids calcium absorption	Rickets
K	Blood clotting	Hemorrhaging

Lack of essential vitamins, which are necessary for health and normal body function, can result in serious illness.

_____

_____

_____

_____

_____

_____

_____

_____

_____

EXERCISE 5-4
Paragraph Writing:
Cause-Effect (Focus on Effect)

Directions: Using cause-effect development, write a paragraph in which you describe the *effects*—negative or positive—that a *teacher* has had on your personality, your feelings about school, or your approach to life in general. Be specific:

1. Mention at least three real effects;
2. Explain each one, using examples, details, or anecdotes.

_____

_____

_____

_____

_____

_____

_____

_____

_____

_____

_____

_____

Construct a *simple list* which shows the organization of your paragraph. Be sure to include a title and at least three items on the list. Do not include such supportive information as examples, details, etc.:

The effects that _____ has had on my life:

1. _____

2. _____

3. _____

CAUSE-EFFECT DEVELOPMENT: FOCUS ON *CAUSE*

Model Paragraph

Why is it that American working women complain about job discrimination? Statistics suggest that there is a basis for their grievances. According to recent figures compiled by the Women's Bureau of the U.S. Department of Labor, nearly 40 percent of all women of working age are in the labor force. Although the median education of all women is higher than that of their male counterparts, women are highly concentrated in underpaid and menial jobs: 75 percent of all clerical workers are women; 55 percent of all service workers are women; 27 percent of all factory workers are women. Of the women with college degrees, 70 percent are working. Of this number, only 2 percent are executives, while 40 percent are employed in clerical, sales, or factory positions. Their median income is only 51 percent of that of men. Only twenty-five states have laws requiring equal pay for equal work, and these laws are often circumvented by giving a woman a lesser title. In contrast, forty-three states have laws which limit the number of hours a woman can work (usually eight) and thereby prevent women from earning overtime pay and promotions. Finally, while the percentage of women in the labor force increases, the income gap between male and female workers has been widening at the rate of ½ percent per year for the past twenty years.

 NOW ASK YOURSELF

1. Which sentence is the topic sentence—the first, the second, or both

    taken together? _____

    Which introduces the idea of cause? _____ Of effect? _____

2. Have any enumerative listing signals been used? _____

3. Is the paragraph in equal, ascending, or descending order? How can you

    tell? _____

4. What kinds of supportive material have been used (examples, details,

    anecdotes, facts and statistics)? _____

    _____

Topic Sentence(s): Why is it that American working women complain about job discrimination? Statistics suggest that there is a basis for their grievances.

CAUSES   EFFECT

Women in general have a higher median education than men, but are employed in menial jobs (clerical, service, factory)

Women with Degrees:

Complaints of Job Discrimination by Women

State Laws:

EXERCISE 5-6
Paragraph Writing:
Cause-Effect Information Transfer

Directions: After studying the diagram, develop a paragraph, using the topic sentences which have been provided.

Topic Sentence(s): When there is a widespread and persistent rise in price and each dollar buys fewer goods and services, *inflation* exists. In one way or another, everyone is to blame for this difficult problem.

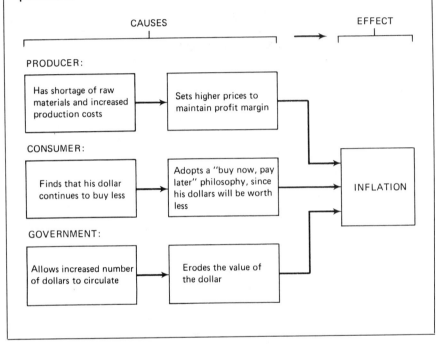

CAUSES   EFFECT

PRODUCER:

| Has shortage of raw materials and increased production costs | → | Sets higher prices to maintain profit margin |

CONSUMER:

| Finds that his dollar continues to buy less | → | Adopts a "buy now, pay later" philosophy, since his dollars will be worth less |

GOVERNMENT:

| Allows increased number of dollars to circulate | → | Erodes the value of the dollar |

INFLATION

EXERCISE 5-7
Paragraph Writing:
Cause-Effect (Focus on Cause)

Directions: Using a cause-effect development, explain why you decided to study at this school. Focus on the various factors which caused you to finally make your decision. You may wish to reread the sample paragraph in Unit One (page 10) before beginning this assignment.

Construct a simple list which will show the organization of your paragraph:

CAUSE-EFFECT DEVELOPMENT:
CHAIN REACTION

Frequently, in developing a causal relationship you will find that the effect of one situation becomes the cause of the next. You have already seen two examples of this—the paragraphs dealing with the effects of television (p. 102) and with the causes of inflation (p. 116). When this relationship exists, we have what is called a *chain reaction*. In other words, the first event leads to or influences the second, the second leads to or influences the third, and so on.

Model Paragraph

For some time now, medical scientists have noted an alarming increase in diseases of the heart and circulation among people who smoke cigarettes. It has been found that the presence of tobacco in the bloodstream causes blood vessels to contract, thus slowing circulation, which eventually leads to hardening of the arteries. As the arteries stiffen, less blood reaches the brain, and the end result of this slowdown is a cerebral hemorrhage, commonly referred to as a "stroke." In addition, tobacco in the bloodstream reduces the ability of the hemoglobin to release oxygen, resulting in shortness of breath. The lack of oxygen forces the heart to beat faster—that is, the pulse rate increases—and in turn accelerates the risk of heart attack.

 *NOW ASK YOURSELF*

1. What is the first cause in the chain? _____

2. What are the *two* final effects? (Notice that there are two chain reactions, both caused by tobacco as it reaches the bloodstream.)

    _____

3. What time words, sentence connectors, or listing signals are used?

    _____

4. What kinds of supportive material are used? _____

    _____

EXERCISE 5-8
Analyzing a Chain-Reaction Paragraph

Topic Sentence: For some time now, medical scientists have noted an alarming increase in diseases of the heart and circulation among those people who smoke cigarettes.

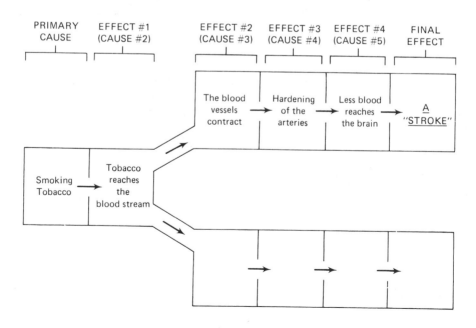

Directions: The following is a random list of causes and effects. Arrange them in a chart of your own (space has been provided following the list). Then write a paragraph based on the information. Your topic sentence will be the following: *For some time now, medical scientists have noted an alarming increase in diseases of the lungs and respiratory tract in people who smoke.*

    a. Impurities can now collect in the windpipe, larynx, and lungs.
    b. In addition to cancer, the lungs may lose their elasticity and cease to function efficiently.
    c. The smoke slows the action of the tiny hairlike projections (*cilia*) which cleanse the air in the windpipe.
    d. Precancerous and cancerous cells form in the various parts of the respiratory tract.
    e. Smoke is inhaled.
    f. With this loss of elasticity, emphysema may develop.
    g. Moreover, since gas, tar, and smoke are no longer removed, they are now allowed to pass through the respiratory tract.

(Hint: The organization of this particular paragraph will resemble that of the previous model paragraph. There are two different chain reactions, each of which finally leads to a different disease.)

Topic Sentence: From some time now, medical scientists have noted an alarming increase in diseases of the lungs and respiratory tract in people who smoke.

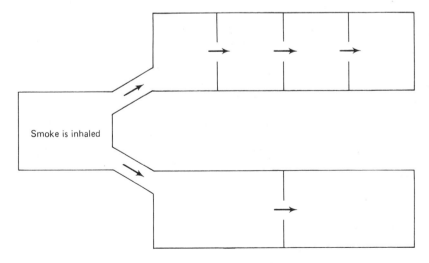

For some time now, medical scientists have noted an alarming increase in diseases of the lungs and respiratory tract in people who smoke.

_____

_____

_____

_____

_____

_____

_____

_____

_____

_____

_____

_____

_____

_____

_____

_____

_____

_____

_____

_____

_____

_____

_____

_____

OPTIONAL WRITING ASSIGNMENTS
(Cause-Effect)

Directions: Develop appropriate paragraphs for any of the five topics below.

Reasons Why People Learn a Foreign Language

Effects of a New Culture Element on Your Society

Effects of Education on an Individual

Which Do You Feel is Most Harmful—Alcohol, Tobacco, or Marijuana? (Choose one and discuss why you feel that it is harmful.)

What Effect Has Living and Studying in the United States Had on You as a Person?

6

SUPPORTING TOPIC SENTENCES

Comparison and Contrast

You may also support your topic sentences by arranging the supporting sentences according to either the *similarities* or the *differences* between two things, or between two aspects of one thing.

COMPARISON: pointing out *likenesses*

CONTRAST: pointing out *differences*

In this chapter, we will examine several of the ways in which comparative and contrastive paragraphs can be organized. We will first take a look at Comparison.

COMPARISON

In the model paragraph which follows, notice that only similarities, or parallels, between the life and death of Kennedy and Lincoln are mentioned. There are obviously many differences between these two men, but the purpose of the paragraph, as it is stated in the topic sentence, is to show the likenesses or similarities between them. In a paragraph of comparison, the differences are often mentioned *only briefly* or are even *omitted entirely*.

Model Paragraph

[1]Are you aware of the striking similarities between two of the most popular U. S. presidents, Abraham Lincoln and John F. Kennedy? [2]A minor point is that the names Lincoln and Kennedy both have seven letters. [3]Both men had their elections legally challenged. [4]Lincoln and Kennedy are both remembered for their sense of humor, as well as for their interest in civil rights. [5]Lincoln became president in 1860; Kennedy, in 1960. [6]Lincoln's secretary was Mrs. Kennedy; Kennedy's secretary was Mrs. Lincoln. [7]Neither man took the advice of his secretary not to make a public appearance on the day on which he was assassinated. [8]Lincoln and Kennedy were both killed on a Friday in the presence of their wives. [9]Both assassins, John Wilkes Booth and Lee Harvey Oswald, have fifteen letters in their names, and both were murdered before they could be brought to trial. [10]Just as Lincoln was succeeded by a Southern Democrat named Johnson, so was Kennedy. [11]Andrew Johnson (Lincoln's successor) was born in 1808; Lyndon Johnson (Kennedy's successor) was born in 1908. [12]And finally, the same caisson carried the bodies of both men in their funeral processions.

NOW ASK YOURSELF

1. Why are no differences mentioned in the paragraph? _____

   _____

2. What is the one key word in the topic sentence which controls the

   development of the paragraph? _____

3. What two words are repeated continually? _____   _____

4. Do you find any examples of pronoun reference? Underline all pronouns and draw arrows to the words they represent.

5. What kinds of supportive materials are used (examples, details, anec-

   dotes, facts and statistics)? _____

   _____

Directions: Reread the model paragraph carefully. Then, in the chart below, indicate the *basis of comparison* in each sentence (i.e., tell which similarity is being discussed), as well as the *comparative words* which have been used.

SENTENCE	BASIS OF COMPARISON	COMPARATIVE STRUCTURES
2	Number of letters in their names	The names Kennedy and Lincoln both have
3	Elections challenged	Both men
4		
5		
6		
7		
8		
9		
10		
11		
12		

STRUCTURES OF COMPARISON

In addition to *listing signals* and the enumerator *similarities,* certain other basic structures are commonly used in writing paragraphs of comparison. There are six basic types.

I. ADJECTIVE/PREPOSITION

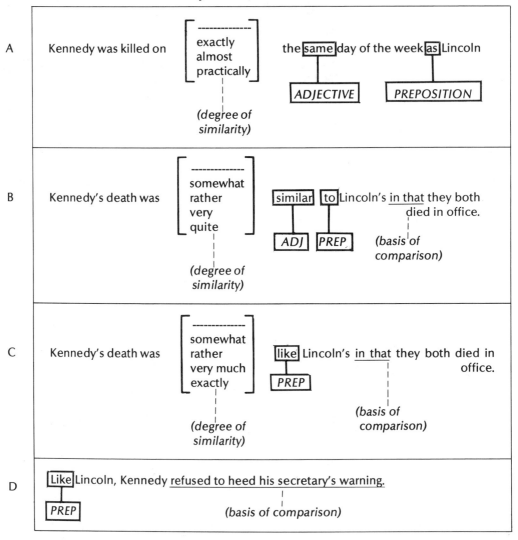

NOW ASK YOURSELF

1. Which of the above structures—A, B, or C—does *not* contain an adjective? _____

2. What is the difference between *same* and *similar*? _____

   _____

3. Which group—A, B, C, or D—allows for the possibility of an *introductory* prepositional phrase? _____

II. ATTACHED STATEMENTS

A

Kennedy was succeeded by a Southern Democrat,	[and] Lincoln was [too.] / [and so] was Lincoln.
Kennedy could arouse the sympathy of the public,	[and] Lincoln could [too.] / [and so] could Lincoln.
Mrs. Kennedy witnessed her husband's assassination,	[and] Mrs. Lincoln did [too.] / [and so] did Mrs. Lincoln.

B

Kennedy's assassin was not brought to trial,	[and] Lincoln's wasn't [either.] / [and neither] was Lincoln's.
Kennedy's secretary couldn't prevent her president's assassination,	[and] Lincoln's couldn't [either.] / [and neither] could Lincoln.
Kennedy didn't finish his term of office,	[and] Lincoln didn't [either.] / [and neither] did Lincoln.

 NOW ASK YOURSELF

1. What kinds of statements are joined by *and . . . too* and *and so*? _____
   What happens to the second subject and verb when *and so* is used?

   _____

2.   What kinds of statements are joined by *and . . . either* and *and neither?*

_____

What happens to the second subject and verb when *and neither* is used?

_____

3.   What part of the verb is repeated in the second part of the sentence

if there is an auxiliary *was?* _____

if the auxiliary is *could?* _____

if there is no auxiliary? _____

III. CORRELATIVE CONJUNCTIONS

A
> [Both] Kennedy [and] Lincoln
> Kennedy [and] Lincoln [both]   had their elections legally challenged.

B
> [Neither] Kennedy's wife [nor] his children were expecting anything unusual to happen that day.
>
> [Neither] Kennedy's children [nor] his wife was expecting anything unusual to happen that day.

C
> [Just as] Lincoln died in office, [so] Kennedy was still president when he was assassinated.

NOW ASK YOURSELF

1.   In the example sentences for *neither . . . nor*, why are the verbs different

(*was, were*)? _____

2.   In C, what does the structure *so Kennedy was still president* remind you

of from "Attached Statements"? _____ What joining element is

missing? _____ Compare *subject-verb word order.* _____

IV. PREDICATE STRUCTURES {TO RESEMBLE / TO HAVE (NOUN) IN COMMON / THERE ARE SIMILARITIES}

A

Kennedy's popularity
[
vaguely
closely
greatly
]
etc.
resembled Lincoln's.

Kennedy *resembled* Lincoln *in that* they were both popular presidents.

B

Kennedy and Lincoln *have*
[certain / many / several / two / etc.]
[things / features / aspects / characteristics / qualities / attitudes / etc.]
in common.

C

There are
[certain / many / several / two / etc.]
similarities between Kennedy and Lincoln.

➤ *NOW ASK YOURSELF*

1. Which of the above structures—A, B, or C—seems most appropriate for showing a *single* similarity? _____

2. Which might make a better topic sentence for a paragraph which included *many* areas of comparison? _____ _____

3. In A, where is the *basis* of comparison indicated in each of the two sentences? _____
Which of the two seems to be more appropriate for giving detailed information? _____

131

Why? (Can you think of a *grammatical* reason?) _____

_____

V. SENTENCE CONNECTORS

Andrew Johnson was born in 1808;	similarly, correspondingly, likewise, in the same way, by the same token,	Lyndon Johnson was born in 1908.

 NOW ASK YOURSELF

1. Can you rewrite this sentence, using one of the suggested connectors, as two separate sentences?

_____

_____

2. From the point of view of punctuation, do these connectors remind you of any others that we have studied so far? Be precise: give examples and page numbers.

_____

_____

VI. PUNCTUATION ONLY

A	Andrew Johnson was born in 1808; Lyndon Johnson was born in 1908.
B	Andrew Johnson was born in 1808; Lyndon Johnson, in 1908.

 NOW ASK YOURSELF

What missing element does the comma replace in Sentence B?

_____

Paraphrasing Sentences of Comparison

Directions: The following sentences are based on the model paragraph (the similarities between Lincoln and Kennedy). Rewrite each of the sentences in two different ways, using the words or phrases which have been indicated. Refer to the charts as often as necessary if you need help. Pay attention to *punctuation.*

1. A minor point is that the names Kennedy and Lincoln both have seven letters.

   (and so/and ... too) _____

   _____

   (both ... and) _____

   _____

2. John Wilkes Booth and Lee Harvey Oswald were murdered before they could be brought to trial.

   (Neither ... nor) _____

   _____

   (like ... in that) _____

   _____

3. Neither man took the advice of his secretary on the day when he was killed.

   (and neither/and ... either) _____

   _____

   (similarly) _____

   _____

4. The same caisson carried the bodies of both men in their funeral processions.

(similar to . . . in that) _____

_____

(Hint: make *funeral* the subject.)

(resembled . . . in that) _____

_____

5. Lincoln became president in 1860, Kennedy in 1960.

(similar to . . . in that) _____

_____

(similarly) _____

_____

6. Lincoln's secretary was Mrs. Kennedy, and Kennedy's secretary was Mrs. Lincoln.

(just as . . . so) _____

_____

(;) _____

_____

EXERCISE 6-3
Comparative Information Transfer

Directions: After studying the chart, develop a paragraph, using the topic sentence which has been provided. Use the structure indicated for each point of comparison.

Topic Sentence: Although men and apes do not look alike at first glance, they share a number of remarkably similar anatomical features.

BASES OF COMPARISON	COMPARATIVE STRUCTURES
Bone structure (skeleton)	"both _____ and _____"
Brain arrangement and shape	"exactly the same"
Light-colored skin	"_____, and so _____" or: "_____, and _____ too"
Hair which grays with aging	"Just as _____, so _____."
Susceptibility to such illnesses as tuberculosis and cancer	"_____; likewise, _____."

_____

_____

_____

_____

_____

_____

_____

_____

_____

_____

_____

_____

_____

EXERCISE 6-4
Paragraph Writing: Comparison

Directions: Compare two people you know who are *very similar.*

_____

_____

_____

_____

_____

_____

_____

CONTRAST

Notice that in the following model paragraph, the author concentrates on the *differences* between extreme extroversion and extreme introversion. He has not denied, however, that most people are a combination of both of these; on the contrary, the expression *a scale* suggests precisely such a combination.

Model Paragraph

[1]According to the Swiss psychiatrist Carl Gustav Jung, every person's personality can be placed somewhere on a scale running from extreme *extroversion* (i.e., an outgoing personality) to extreme *introversion* (i.e., a withdrawn personality). [2]The typical extrovert is particularly fond of people and people-oriented activities: he is sociable, likes parties, has many friends, needs to have people to talk to, and does not like reading

or studying by himself. ³The typical introvert, on the other hand, is a quiet, retiring sort of person, introspective, fond of books rather than people. ⁴Unlike the extrovert, who craves excitement, takes chances, and is generally impulsive, the introvert shuns excitement, takes matters of everyday life with proper seriousness, and likes a well-ordered mode of life. ⁵Whereas the extrovert tends to be aggressive and loses his temper easily, the introvert tends to keep his feelings under close control, seldom behaves in an aggressive manner, and does not lose his temper easily. ⁶The introvert is more reliable and less optimistic than the extrovert. ⁷The extrovert may often be subject to criminal or psychopathic behavior, in contrast to the introvert, who may exhibit neurotic tendencies. ⁸A further difference between the two involves the ability to remember: studies have tended to show that the extrovert learns faster than the introvert but, in the end, remembers less.[1]

NOW ASK YOURSELF

1. Why are no similarities mentioned in the model paragraph? _____

    _____

2. What part of the topic sentence prepares the reader to expect a para-

    graph of contrast development? _____

3. What two words are repeated continually? _____   _____

4. Do you find any examples of pronoun reference? Underline all pronouns and draw arrows to the words they represent.

5. Are any *listing signals* used? _____

    _____

6. What kinds of supportive materials are used (examples, details, anec-

    dotes, facts and statistics)? _____

    _____

    _____

    _____

[1]Nicholas Wright, ed., *Understanding Human Behaviour* (London: Phoebus Publishing Company/BPC Publishing, Limited, 1974), pp. 54–56.

EXERCISE 6-5
Analyzing a Paragraph of Contrast

Directions: Reread the sample paragraph carefully. Then, in the chart below, indicate which contrast words have been used for each area of contrast. Also note briefly the differences themselves.

SENTENCE	BASES OF CONTRAST		CONTRASTIVE
	Extrovert	Introvert	STRUCTURES
2,3	(Sociability)		On the other hand
	Fond of people: sociable, likes parties, etc.	Prefers books to people, is shy and retiring	
4	(Risk taking)		
5	(Expression of feelings, aggression)		
6	(Reliability, optimism)		
7	(	)	
8	(	)	

STRUCTURES OF CONTRAST

I. -ER . . . THAN; MORE . . . THAN; LESS . . . THAN;
AS . . . AS

A.	1. The introvert	is quieter than is *more* reliable *than* is *less* optimistic *than* learns *more* slowly *than*	2. the extrovert.
B.	2. The extrovert	isn't as quiet as isn't as reliable as doesn't learn as slowly as	1. the introvert.
	1. The introvert	isn't as optimistic as	2. the extrovert.

▶ *NOW ASK YOURSELF*

1. What kinds of words are used with -*er . . . than?* _____

    With *more . . . than* and *less . . . than?* _____

2. When can *as . . . as* be used to indicate contrast? (Remember that it can

    also indicate similarity!) _____

3. Can you rewrite the second sentence in Group B, keeping the meaning
    the same but changing the order of *extrovert* and *introvert?*

    "The extrovert _____"

II. PREPOSITIONS

Unlike Contrary to As opposed to	the extrovert, who craves excitement, the introvert likes a well- ordered mode of life.

*Basis of
contrast*

III. ADVERBIAL CLAUSES

⎡Although⎤
⎢Whereas⎥ the extrovert loses his temper quickly, the introvert seldom does.
⎣While ⎦

basis of
contrast

➤ *NOW ASK YOURSELF*

Can you rewrite the sentence in the following ways?

1. Although the introvert _____

   _____

2. Unlike the _____, who _____

   _____, the _____

IV. VERBAL STRUCTURES

The introvert ⎡contrasts *with* ⎤ the extrovert ⎰ in regard to ⎱ his ability to
               ⎢differs *from* ⎥   ⎱ in respect to ⎰ remember.
               ⎣is different *from*⎦

basis of
contrast

➤ *NOW ASK YOURSELF*

1. Can the "basis of contrast" be explained more fully by using a structure from this group or by using an adverbial clause, as was done in Group III?

   _____

2. Could the basis of contrast be explained more fully by using *in that* instead of *in regard to*? _____

   _____

3. Can you expand the sentence from the above box by following these indications?

    "The introvert differs from the extrovert in that the extrovert

    _____

    _____

    whereas the introvert _____

    _____."

    What two groups of contrast structures does this new sentence combine?

    _____ and _____

V. SENTENCE CONNECTORS

A	The extrovert loves crowds;	however, on the other hand, in contrast,	the introvert is fond of solitude.

basis of
contrast

B	The extrovert loves crowds; the introvert,	however, on the other hand, in contrast,	is fond of solitude.

NOW ASK YOURSELF

1. How does the punctuation of the above two sentences differ? _____

    _____

2. Can you rewrite *each* of them as two separate sentences?

    a. _____

        _____

    b. _____

        _____

VI. PUNCTUATION ONLY

A	The introvert likes books; the extrovert is fond of people.
B	The introvert likes books; the extrovert, people

EXERCISE 6-6
Paraphrasing Sentences of Contrast

Directions: The following sentences are based on the model paragraph (the differences between the typical extrovert and the typical introvert). Rewrite each of the sentences in two different ways, using words or phrases from the sentence, as well as the structure of contrast which has been indicated. Refer back to the boxes as often as necessary. Pay attention to *punctuation.*

1. Studies have tended to show that the extrovert learns faster than the introvert but, in the end, remembers less.

    (however,-form B) <u>Studies have tended to show that the extrovert</u>

    <u>learns faster than the introvert; in the end, however, he remembers less.</u>

    (although) _____

    _____

2. Unlike the extrovert, who takes chances and is generally impulsive, the introvert shuns excitement.

    (differs from . . . in that . . . whereas) _____

    _____

    _____

    (more/-er . . . than) _____

    _____

3. The typical extrovert is particularly fond of parties and people-oriented activities; in contrast, the typical introvert is a quiet, introspective sort of person.

(unlike ... who) _____

_____

_____

(while) _____

_____

_____

4. The extrovert may be subject to criminal or psychopathic behavior, in
    contrast to the introvert, who may exhibit neurotic tendencies.

    (differ from ... in that ... whereas) _____

    _____

    (on the other hand—form B) _____

    _____

5. Whereas the extrovert tends to be aggressive and loses his temper
    quickly, the introvert seldom behaves in an aggressive manner and keeps
    his feelings under close control.

    (unlike ... who) _____

    _____

    _____

    °(contrast with ... in regard to) _____

    _____

    _____

METHODS OF CONTRAST

There are two main ways in which to organize your material when you wish
to develop a contrast paragraph. The first method has been used in the
preceding model paragraph (the typical extrovert vs. the typical introvert).

In this method, the contrasts are made one at a time, or *point by point.* Thus, the two personality types are first contrasted for sociability, then for risk taking, and so on. Note, in the preceding model paragraph, that the words *extrovert* and *introvert* are repeated each time a new area of contrast is brought up:

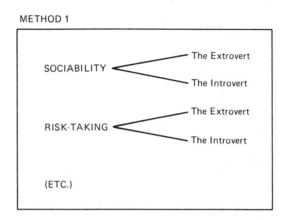

The writer could, of course, have *completely described* the extrovert, then, in the second part of the paragraph, have gone on to *completely describe* the introvert. This would have given a very different-looking, but equally acceptable paragraph:

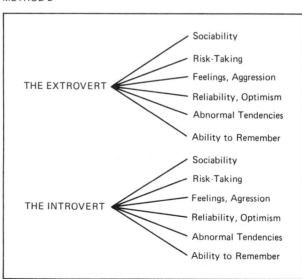

The following is an example of Method II (completely describing one thing, then completely describing the other):

In studying the phenomenon usually referred to as sleep, we are actually dealing with more than one phenomenon. In point of fact, we spend the night alternating between two different types of sleep, each with different brain mechanisms and different purposes. As a person falls asleep, his brain waves develop a slower and less regular pattern than in a waking state. This is called *orthodox* sleep. In this state the brain is apparently resting. Its blood supply is reduced, and its temperature falls slightly. Breathing and heart rate are regular. The muscles remain slightly tensed. After about an hour in this state, however, the brain waves begin to show a more active pattern again, even though the person is apparently asleep very deeply. This is called *paradoxical* sleep because it has much in common with being awake. Paradoxical (active) sleep is marked by irregular breathing and heart rate, increased blood supply to the brain, and increased brain temperature. Most of the muscles are relaxed. There are various jerky movements of the body and face, including short bursts of rapid eye movement (REM's), which indicate that we are dreaming. Thus, we spend the night alternating between these two vital "restoration jobs": working on the brain (paradoxical sleep) and working on the body (orthodox sleep.)[2]

NOW ASK YOURSELF

1. Is the *first* or the *second* sentence the topic sentence? Or is it *both* of

    them? (Explain your answer.) _____

    _____

    _____

2. What *contrast structures* do you find in the paragraph? _____

    _____

    Which type of contrast—Method I or Method II—seems to require more

    structures of contrast? _____ Why? _____

    _____

[2]*Ibid.,* pp. 23–24.

3. Are all of the following bases of contrast referred to in both orthodox and paradoxical sleep? Check each box as you find the information. Two boxes should be empty.

	ORTHODOX	PARADOXICAL
Brain waves (speed and regularity)		
Amount of blood (blood supply)		
Temperature		
Breathing, heart rate		
Muscle tension		
Body and face movements		
Rapid eye movements		

If you were writing a contrastive paragraph but did not have complete information on one of the things you were contrasting, which method

would you choose? Why? _____

ADDITIONAL COMMENTS ON THE TOPIC SENTENCE

You were told in Unit One that most paragraphs begin with a topic sentence (see p. 3). However, since then you have seen two examples of something you will encounter in English—*two* beginning sentences which carry the main idea of the paragraph. The first paragraph was on p. 113:

Why is it that American working women complain about job discrimination? Statistics suggest that there is a basis for their grievances.

You will notice that the first sentence introduces the idea in a general way, wondering why women complain. The second sentence goes further and notes that there *are* reasons, and that these reasons are verifiable through statistics. The paragraph then goes on to present these statistics to the reader.

At this point there is no reason why you should try to write paragraphs which begin with these "double topic sentences." Nevertheless, you must learn to be aware of them while you are reading; otherwise, you may miss the point which the author is trying to make.

 NOW ASK YOURSELF

In the paragraph on p. 146, which deals with the differences between orthodox and paradoxical sleep, what is the relationship between the first two sentences? Try to explain in your own words.

_____

_____

_____

_____

EXERCISE 6-7
Analyzing Paragraphs of Contrast

Directions: Read the paragraph on the two types of sleep again carefully, then fill in the chart below in fairly detailed fashion.

TOPIC SENTENCES	
ORTHODOX SLEEP	Brain waves—slower, less regular
	Blood supply
	Temperature
	Breathing, heart rate
	Muscle tension
	Body and face movements
	Rapid eye movements

	Brain waves
PARADOXICAL SLEEP	Blood supply
	Temperature
	Breathing, heart rate
	Muscle tension
	Body and face movements
	Rapid eye movements
CONCLUSION	

EXERCISE 6-8
Reordering Paragraphs of Contrast

Directions: Take the paragraph on sleep (Method II) and rewrite it according to Method I (point-by-point). Use as many contrast expressions as necessary.

_____

_____

_____

_____

_____

_____

_____

_____

_____

_____

_____

_____

_____

_____

_____

_____

_____

_____

_____

_____

_____

_____

_____

_____

*EXERCISE 6-9
Analyzing and Reordering Paragraphs of Contrast

Directions: Read the following paragraph, which is organized according to Method I (point-by-point). Fill in the chart on the next page. Then rewrite the paragraph according to Method II (completely describe the first; then completely describe the second).

[1]Although the classless society is still a myth, the distinctions and barriers between classes are fewer in the United States than in many more traditional parts of the world. [2]Whereas in the old world, class is legal and hereditary, in the United States it is neither. [3]In the old world, too, it is quite impersonal: you are what you are, and that is the end of it. [4]On the contrary, in America it is wholly personal; each person carves out his own economic position, just as he carves out his own social position. [5]Nor is the job ever finished once and for all; as the individual can move upward on the social scale, so he can move downward. [6]In the United States neither wealth, family, nor formal position provides any guarantee, though collectively they do provide indications of social

standing. [7]In parts of Europe and Asia, a government official has a kind of automatic right to deference and prestige, and he is deemed worthy of respect until proved otherwise. [8]The opposite is true in America. [9]One does not command respect or honor merely on the basis of his title; it is well to remember that the title of the President of the United States is "Mr. President," and that all Harvard professors are called "Mister." [10]A judge may be "Your Honor" and a clergyman "Reverend," but the judge will not receive honor nor the clergyman reverence unless he merits it. [11]Money can, of course, buy special favors—the best seats in a restaurant, the best service in a hotel—but it cannot buy deference. [12]In other lands, too, class commonly has outward symbols: dress, manner, speech, accent, school, church affiliation, unlike the U.S., where these indices are of little or no importance, and anyone who tried to apply them would go badly astray.[3]

SENTENCE	BASES OF CONTRAST		GRAMMATICAL STRUCTURE(S)
	The old world	*The United States*	
2	(nature of class)		whereas
	Legal, hereditary	Neither legal nor hereditary	
3,4,5,6	(Personal vs. impersonal; stability)		
7,8,9 10,11	(Title vs. respect)		
12	(Visible symbols of class)		

[3]Adapted from Henry Steel Commager, *Meet the U.S.A.* (New York: Institute of International Education, 1970), p. 87.

Method II

_ _

_ _

_ _

_ _

	BASES OF CONTRAST
THE OLD WORLD	Nature of class
	Personal vs. impersonal; stability
	Title vs. respect
	Visible symbols of class:
THE UNITED STATES	Nature of class
	Personal vs. impersonal; stability
	Title vs. respect
	Visible symbols of class:

EXERCISE 6-10
Paragraph Writing:
Contrastive Information Transfer

Directions: Referring back to the population graph and exercise (p. 37), contrast urbanization in India with that in England and Wales. Notice that your topic sentence must reflect the fact that this paragraph contrasts the two. State the method you have used.

_____

_____

_____

_____

_____

_____

_____

_____

_____

_____

_____

_____

_____

_____

_____

_____ _____ _____ _____ _____ _____ _____ _____ _____ _____ _____ _____

_____ _____ _____ _____ _____ _____ _____ _____ _____ _____ _____

_____ _____ _____ _____ _____ _____ _____ _____ _____ _____ _____

_____ _____ _____ _____ _____ _____ _____ _____ _____ _____ _____

(METHOD USED:)

EXERCISE 6-11
Paragraph Writing:
Contrast

Directions: Write a paragraph in which you *contrast* two people you know who are very *different.* Indicate at the end which method you have used— Method I (point-by-point contrast) or Method II (separate sections).

_____ _____ _____ _____ _____ _____ _____ _____ _____ _____ _____

_____ _____ _____ _____ _____ _____ _____ _____ _____ _____ _____

_____ _____ _____ _____ _____ _____ _____ _____ _____ _____ _____

_____ _____ _____ _____ _____ _____ _____ _____ _____ _____ _____

_____ _____ _____ _____ _____ _____ _____ _____ _____ _____ _____

_____ _____ _____ _____ _____ _____ _____ _____ _____ _____ _____

_____ _____ _____ _____ _____ _____ _____ _____ _____ _____ _____

_____ _____ _____ _____ _____ _____ _____ _____ _____ _____ _____

_____ _____ _____ _____ _____ _____ _____ _____ _____ _____ _____

_____ _____ _____ _____ _____ _____ _____ _____ _____ _____ _____

_____ _____ _____ _____ _____ _____ _____ _____ _____ _____ _____

_____ _____ _____ _____ _____ _____ _____ _____ _____ _____ _____

— — — — — — — — — — — — — — — — — — —

— — — — — — — — — — — — — — — — — — —

— — — — — — — — — — — — — — — — — — —

— — — — — — — — — — — — — — — — — — —

— — — — — — — — — — — — — — — — — — —

— — — — — — — — — — — — — — — — — — —

— — — — — — — — — — — — — — — — — — —

— — — — — — — — — — — — — — — — — — —

— — — — — — — — — — — — — — — — — — —

— — — — — — — — — — — — — — — — — — —

— — — — — — — — — — — — — — — — — — —

(METHOD USED: _____) ___ — ___ —

COMPARISON *AND* CONTRAST

You have no doubt realized that when you are showing similarities between two things, you will almost always find differences as well. The converse is equally true: most things being contrasted will also have similarities. This is the case with the following model paragraphs.

Model Paragraphs

[1]When listening to a conversation between an American and an Englishman, a person will become aware of the most significant differences between the two varieties of the English language. [2]While the Englishman does not pronounce *r* sounds before a consonant sound or

at the end of a word, the American does. [3]This might lead to a rather humorous misunderstanding if, when asked by the American what his job was, the Englishman answered that he was a *clerk* (pronounced *clock* to the American ear). [4]Failure to use the *r* sound at the end of a word might also lead to confusion between words like *paw* and *pour*. [5]Moreover, a noticeable difference exists between the basic words used to express the same thing. [6]The American might want to know the price of *gas* in London, but the Englishman will answer him by using the word *petrol*. [7]Unlike the American, who wears an *undershirt* when the weather is cold, the Englishman wears a *vest*. [8]The American wants to know where the *elevator* is, while the Englishman asks the location of the *lift*.

[9]The similarities found in this hypothetical conversation, however, will far outweigh the differences. [10]The meanings of most words are, of course, exactly the same. [11]The pronunciation of the consonant sounds, the rhythm, stress, and intonation systems in both American and British English closely resemble each other. [12]In grammar, the similarities are numerous. [13]British English makes a distinction between count and mass nouns, and so does American English. [14]They both have the same verb and tense systems. [15]The grammar of both languages is similar in that they both form and compare adjectives and adverbs in the same way. [16]In fact, the similarities between the two languages—or, more precisely, between these two forms of the same language—are such that there is rarely any serious breakdown in communication between an American speaker and a British speaker.

EXERCISE 6-12
Analyzing Paragraphs of
Comparison *and* Contrast

Directions: After carefully rereading the model paragraphs on the differences and similarities between American and British English, fill in the two charts which follow.

PARAGRAPH 1 (differences)

Topic Sentence: _____

_____

_____

SENTENCE	BASES OF CONTRAST		CONTRASTIVE STRUCTURES
	American	British	
2	Pronunciation r pronounced be- fore consonants and at ends of words	not pronounced	while
3	(example)		
4	(example)		
5	Certain vocabulary items		
6	(example)		
7	(example)		
8	(example)		

PARAGRAPH 2 (similarities)

Topic Sentence: _____

_____

_____

SENTENCE	BASES OF COMPARISON	COMPARATIVE STRUCTURES
10		
11		
12		
13		
14		
15		

THE "SPLIT" TOPIC SENTENCE

In the preceding exercise you were asked to find a topic sentence for each of the two paragraphs. However, these two paragraphs go together, since their combined purpose is to show similarities *and* differences. Therefore, in a very real sense the meanings of their two topic sentences go together, even though they are physically separated from each other.

REMEMBER THIS

The main idea may be carried by *one or more* sentences.

They may be *together* (in the case of a single paragraph) or *"split"* (in the case of more than one paragraph).

Thus, the complete main idea for the preceding model paragraphs is as follows:

When listening to a conversation between an American and an Englishman, a person will become aware of the most significant differences between the two varieties of the English language. _____

_____

_____

_____

The similarities found in this hypothetical conversation, however, will far outweigh the differences. _____

_____

_____

_____

This is important for you to know, particularly when you are reading. Otherwise, you might miss the fact that there are both similarities *and* differences, and that the similarities are *far more numerous and important.*

160

EXERCISE 6-13
Paragraph Writing:
Comparison and Contrast

Directions: Below are brief descriptions of the typical person born under each astrological sign. Using the day of the month on which you were born, find and carefully read the description of your sign. After studying the description, write two paragraphs in which you both *compare* and *contrast* your personality as you see it with the description of the sign. (You will no doubt agree with part of the description; you may also find that parts of the description do not correspond to your image of yourself.)

Be *specific* when illustrating the similarities and differences that you mention. Give good examples.

Use the "split" topic sentence technique which has been explained to you. Decide whether the similarities or the differences are more significant; put them last (ascending order).

ARIES (March 22 to April 20)

The characteristic Aries type has an impulsive, adventurous spirit. He possesses unlimited energy and hates restrictions almost as much as he loves freedom. Because of this, he is frequently impatient and lacking in subtlety. He is sometimes selfish and is easily angered. He is quick to put his personal goals first.

TAURUS (April 21 to May 21)

The Taurean is characterized by stability, reliability, and patience. He is tolerant and at the same time strong-willed. He is persistent in all his endeavors, especially business. He loves all of the finer things of life: good food, pleasant surroundings, and luxuries in general. At times he can be very stubborn and fixed in his ways and opinions. He is generally lacking in flexibility and in originality.

GEMINI (May 22 to June 22)

Resourcefulness, creativity, and versatility are attributed to the Gemini. He is also spontaneous, talkative, inquisitive, and amusing. At times, however, he has difficulty controlling his nervous energy and becomes restless, inconsistent, and two-faced.

CANCER (June 23 to July 23)

The Cancer, who is extremely sensitive, sympathetic, and creative, is devoted to humanitarian principles. He is extremely devoted to family and home. Because he is emotionally resourceful, he gives the outward impression of being impenetrable and self-assured, while in reality he may be hypersensitive and moody. He is somewhat unstable and can tend toward self-pity.

LEO (July 24 to August 23)

Generosity of mind and spirit characterize the Leo. He is a born leader who enjoys the dramatic and "doing things in a big way." He is proud, creative, and faithful to friends and family. He is fully aware of his positive traits, which may lead him to becoming dogmatic, intolerant, pompous, and even bullying.

VIRGO (August 24 to September 23)

The Virgo possesses remarkable powers of discrimination and analysis. He is meticulous, discrete, and extremely honest. He enjoys hard work and always does it in a thorough, methodical way. He is able to render constructive criticism, but, because he is so precise and fastidious, he may become hypercritical. He pays so much attention to detail that he tends to be a worrier.

LIBRA (September 24 to October 23)

The Libra, who prizes harmony above all else, is charming, easygoing, and cooperative. He is refined and diplomatic by nature. He cannot be happy in an environment where there is discord, and this frequently results in his being indecisive, changeable, and dependent on others to take responsibility for decisions. He is a great procrastinator.

SCORPIO (October 24 to November 22)

Possessing powerful feelings and emotions, the Scorpio is discerning, subtle, and extremely imaginative. He has a strong sense of purpose and will persist until that purpose is accomplished. The Scorpio is so self-controlled that he may even seem secretive or suspicious to others. He is loyal to friends, but resentful and vindictive if he feels that they have "crossed" him.

162

SAGITTARIUS (November 23 to December 22)

The popular Sagittarius has an optimistic, philosophical attitude toward life. A freedom-lover, he is dependable, jovial, and sincere. His frankness may lead him to be tactless. He has a tendency toward exaggeration, boisterousness, and extremism.

CAPRICORN (December 23 to January 19)

The reliable, ambitious, prudent Capricorn is capable of achieving his goals patiently through determined effort. He is careful to take advantage of every opportunity offered to him. He is somewhat pessimistic and conventional in his outlook and can sometimes be rigid and miserly.

AQUARIUS (January 20 to February 19)

Friendly, idealistic, and original, the Aquarius has an independent, reforming spirit and a progressive outlook. He is intellectually inclined and always ready to use his talents for the improvement of society as a whole. His idealism may cause him to become rebellious and eventually distort his vision of reality. At those times, he is unpredictable and eccentric.

PISCES (February 20 to March 21)

The Pisces is sympathetic, sensitive, and generous. Intuitive and emotional, he is capable of great warmth and compassion toward others. Because he is so impressionable, he may sometimes be weak-willed, indecisive, and completely impractical in coping with day-to-day routine.

7 DEFINITION

In formal writing, it is sometimes necessary to write a paragraph to explain what a term means or how you are using it in a particular situation. This is called a paragraph of definition. A paragraph of definition may be either a *formal* definition, which explains the meaning as you might find it in the dictionary, or a *stipulated* definition, which explains how you are using a particular term within a specific context. In both cases, you will notice that definition often involves a combination of the kinds of development we have been studying in the previous four chapters.

THE FORMAL DEFINITION

Model Definition

A wristwatch is a mechanical time-telling device
which is worn on a band about the wrist.

As you can see, a formal definition includes three kinds of things: the term to be defined, the class to which a thing belongs, and the features which distinguish it from other things in that class. In the case of a wristwatch:

Term = wristwatch

Class = device

Distinguishing features = 1) mechanical
2) for telling time
3) worn on a band about the wrist

Thus, it is distinguished from nonmechanical time-telling devices (e.g., sundials) and other kinds of mechanical ones (e.g., alarm clocks).

A diagram of the information might look like this:

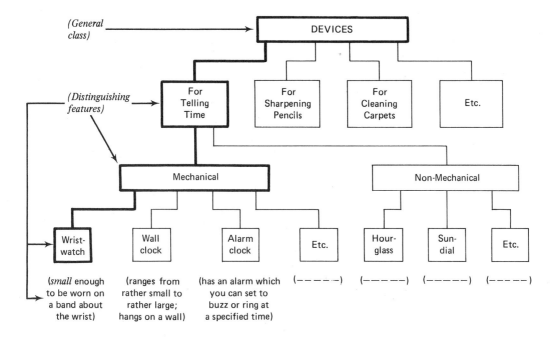

EXERCISE 7-1
Categorization (Formal Definition)

Directions: Below is a chart with ten terms. Fill in the chart for each of the terms. Then write one-sentence formal definitions for *five* of them.

TERM	GENERAL CLASS	DISTINGUISHING FEATURES
A cafeteria	Restaurant	Self-service
A pencil		
A rose		

TERM	GENERAL CLASS	DISTINGUISHING FEATURES
The metric system		
A joke		
A canoe		
Zinc		
A loveseat		
A carrot		
A laundromat		

Definitions

1. _____

   _____

2. _____

   _____

3. _____

   _____

4. _____

   _____

5. _____

   _____

SHORT PARAGRAPHS OF EXTENDED DEFINITION

When the general class and distinguishing features have been given, the writer may then go on to expand or *extend* his formal definition by giving additional information about the term being defined. This might include such things as a physical description or a list of the advantages of the item. In the case of a wristwatch, for instance, the writer might want to comment on variety in appearance and popularity. Notice the following paragraph on the wristwatch, where all of this information has been included.

A wristwatch is a mechanical device which is used for telling time. Its main advantage over other types of time-telling devices (such things as clocks, sundials, or hourglasses) is that it is small enough to be worn on the wrist, so that one can easily know the time by looking down. Wristwatches come in various shapes and sizes, but all have one thing in common: a band or strap with which they may be attached to the wrist. In the United States, where "time is money," practically everyone wears a wristwatch.

 NOW ASK YOURSELF

In which sentence of the preceding paragraph do you find evidence of the following:

1. Enumeration? _____

2. Cause-effect? _____

3. Comparison-contrast? _____

4. Examples-details? _____

EXERCISE 7-2
Paragraph Writing:
Definitional Information Transfer

Directions: Referring back to Exercise 7-1, choose *two* of the formal definitions which you wrote and develop each of them into a short paragraph of extended definition. Be prepared to explain *how* you have extended or expanded your original definition:

Purpose or use

Physical description

Various kinds or types

Advantages or disadvantages

Historically interesting information

PROBLEMS IN DEFINITION

THE CIRCULAR DEFINITION

There are three common problems which may arise in writing definitions. The first problem is that of the *circular definition*, in which the term being defined is repeated in the definition (either the word itself or a word from the same family). For example, if you define "economics" as "the study of the economy," you have written a circular definition:

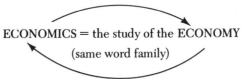

ECONOMICS = the study of the ECONOMY
(same word family)

THE OVER-EXTENDED DEFINITION

A second frequent problem is the *overextended definition*, in which the definition can be applied to more things than just the term being defined. If you define "lemonade" as "a refreshing drink," for example, you have over-extended your definition because there are many other things which fall into this category:

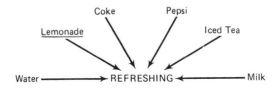

Coke   Pepsi

Lemonade   Iced Tea

Water ⟶ REFRESHING ⟵ Milk

THE OVERRESTRICTED DEFINITION

The third problem area in definition writing is that of *overrestriction*. An overrestricted definition is one in which the term being defined is more comprehensive than the definition (i.e., you restrict the item to only a part of its total definition). For example, defining a "table" as "a place where one eats" is overly restrictive because a table may be used for many other purposes:

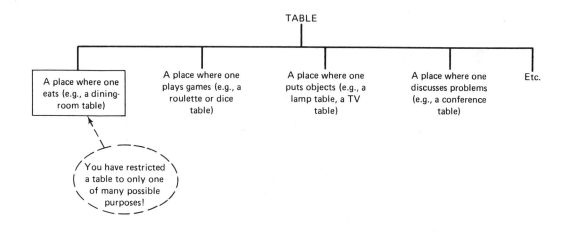

EXERCISE 7-3
Identifying Problems in Definition

Directions: Below are some definitions which do not meet the requirements for a good definition. Explain which problem arises in each. Then rewrite the definition in an acceptable way. Your definitions may be only one or two sentences.

1. A ranch is a place where cowboys live.

    Problem: overrestricted _____

    Your Definition: A ranch is a large farm, particularly in the American

    West, on which large herds of cattle, horses, or sheep are raised.

    _____

2. Oil is a liquid.

    Problem: _____

    Your Definition: _____

    _____

    _____

    _____

3. Inflation is a process whereby money becomes inflated.

   Problem: _____

   Your Definition: _____

   _____

   _____

   _____

4. A boot is a rubber covering for the human foot.

   Problem: _____

   Your Definition: _____

   _____

   _____

   _____

5. A university is a place where people study.

   Problem: _____

   Your Definition: _____

   _____

   _____

   _____

6. A grocery store is a place where people buy food.

   Problem: _____

   Your Definition: _____

   _____

   _____

   _____

7. Art is something found in a museum.

    Problem: _____

    Your Definition: _____

    _____

    _____

    _____

8. Pollution is the process whereby chemicals are dumped into rivers.

    Problem: _____

    Your Definition: _____

    _____

    _____

    _____

9. Language is a means of communication.

    Problem: _____

    Your Definition: _____

    _____

    _____

    _____

10. Democracy is a democratic system of government.

    Problem: _____

    Your Definition: _____

    _____

    _____

    _____

THE STIPULATED DEFINITION

THE FORMAL DEFINITION VS. THE STIPULATED DEFINITION

The second—and more difficult—type of definition which you may be required to write is one in which you explain how you are using a term *for a particular purpose,* or in which you explain *your particular interpretation of the term.* The word, in the sense in which you understand it, may differ from its usual definition. Like the extended formal definition, the stipulated definition is usually longer than a single sentence.

The kinds of words which require this type of definition are generally abstract ideas or qualities such as *friendship, poverty, justice,* and so on. For instance, you may have to begin a longer composition by defining exactly how you will be using a term in that particular paper:

1. Of all the possible dictionary meanings of the term, you will be using only one, and definitely not the others; or

2. You will be using the term in a very special sense, not to be found in the dictionary (in a personal essay, this may mean making clear your own interpretation of a word; in a philosophy course, it may mean giving a clear explanation of how a particular philosopher uses the term).

EXERCISE 7-4
Analyzing Stipulated Definitions

Directions: Read the following three paragraphs of stipulated definition. Answer the questions which follow each paragraph.

I.   The American concept of success has not changed much over the two centuries of its existence. The average American thinks about personal success in terms quite different from the rest of the world. First, it has always meant providing your family with a decent standard of living with some margin of comfort. Second, it means ending your life in a higher and more prosperous position than you began it. To an American, it is clear that success is the result of hard work, self-reliance, and is "God's reward" for American virtue. The lesson that success lay in your own hands became ingrained because it was within the reach of any free man. Because Americans have consistently been "successful" within this meaning of the term, they have not altered this view substantially.[1]

Questions

1. Why is this interpretation of success a *stipulated* definition rather than a formal definition? _____

    _____

2. What is the topic sentence? _____

    _____

3. What type of development is used to support the topic sentence (enumeration, process, chronological order, cause-effect, comparison, contrast)?

    _____

    _____

4. What kinds of supporting material have been used (examples, details, anecdotes, facts and statistics)? _____

    _____

    _____

5. Do you notice any *repetition* of words? _____

    _____

6. What do the following pronouns refer back to in the text? (One of them does not specifically refer back to anything.)

    it (line (4) _____

    it (line 5) _____

    it (line 7) _____

    it (line 7) _____

[1] Adapted from J. W. Anderson, "The Idea of Success," *The Washington Post, July 4, 1976,* p. 62.

it (line 10) _____

this (line 11) _____

they (line 12) _____

this (line 12) _____

II.   When European theorists speak of equality, they commonly mean equal status or equal wealth. When Americans use the same term, they usually mean a competition in which everyone gets an equal start. Most of the great social reforms of the 1960's were designed to bring the poor and the Blacks "into the running" on something approaching the same footing as the more prosperous and better educated majority. Giving everyone the vote, teaching children to read, and getting them all though high school with a real chance of college beyond all represent the kind of equality that has enormous support in the United States. The basic arrangement of economic life has always provided a balance: enough equality to permit new initiative to flourish wherever it might arise and enough inequality to reward it. Nowhere else have the rewards been so rich and the distribution so wide.[2]

Questions

1. Why is this interpretation of equality a *stipulated* definition rather than a

   formal one? _____

   _____

2. What is the topic sentence? (Look at the paragraph carefully.) _____

   _____

   _____

3. What type of development is used to support the topic sentence? _____

   _____

   _____

[2]*Ibid.*, p. 73.

4. What kinds of supporting material have been used (examples, details, anecdotes, facts and statistics)? _____

_____

_____

5. What do the following pronouns refer to:

    they (line 1): _____

    they (line 3): _____

    them (line 8): _____

    it (line 12): _____

*III.   It has been said that by understanding what makes a nation laugh, you can define its people. To Americans, laughter is the great leveler, the crystallizer of our iconoclasm. Jack Kennedy's crack about seeing nothing wrong with appointing his brother Robert to the Cabinet "to give him some legal experience as Attorney General before he goes out to practice law" is an example of the acid touch that is common to American humor. The sense of the comic in the United States centers around our own ridiculousness and around the menace suddenly perceived as no longer threatening. As the popular cartoon character Pogo said: "We have met the enemy and he is us." We tend toward a humor that is fast, frank, and irreverent. A Black comedian tells his predominantly white audience, "We finally made it. The first Black man was indicted for income tax evasion. We finally made it ... into non-violent crime." A more boisterous form of humor is represented by slapstick: a kick in the pants, a pie in the boss's face, the great chase scene where hundreds of people run wildly about, but no one gets caught. Certainly American humor, with its nothing-sacred air and its capacity to hurt and heal, reveals yet another side of the elusive "American character."[3]

[3]Adapted from Shelby Coffey III, "Our Savage Wit," *The Washington Post, July 4, 1976,* p. 166–179.

Questions

1. Why is this interpretation of humor a *stipulated* definition?

   _____

2. Is the first sentence really the topic sentence? Why or why not? _____

   _____

3. What type of development is used to support the topic sentence? _____

   _____

   _____

4. What kinds of supporting material do you find? _____

   _____

   _____

5. What other words in the paragraph are closely related in meaning to the

   word *humor*? _____

6. What do the following pronouns refer to?

   it (line 1): _____

   its (line 2) _____

   him, he (line 5) _____

   it (line 13): _____

   its (line 18) _____

A final note about stipulated definitions is in order. You have no doubt noticed that the stipulated or personal definition lends itself very easily to various kinds of paragraph development (e.g., the previous three paragraphs). This is understandable when you consider the nature of this kind of definition. The writer, as we have said, is defining how *he* is going to be using the particular term. In terms of types of paragraph development, this may mean, for example, that he

1. Will be using the term in several different ways (*enumeration* and/or *contrast*)

2. Will be using the term in a way which differs significantly from the dictionary definition (*contrast*)

3. Will be showing that the explanation of the term has several different parts (*enumeration*)

4. Will be showing how the meaning of the term has changed (*chronological order* and/or *contrast*)

5. Will be writing of *causes* or of *effects* in the course of his explanation

EXERCISE 7-5
Review Exercise:
Identifying Paragraph Types

Directions: Identify the types of paragraph development used in Unit One, Exercise 1-5 (pp. 12–13) and Exercise 1-7 (pp. 18–20).

Unit One, Exercise 1-5	*Unit One, Exercise 1-7*
Paragraph 1: _____	Paragraph 1: _____
Paragraph 2: _____	Paragraph 2: _____
Paragraph 3: _____	Paragraph 3: _____
Paragraph 4: _____	Paragraph 4: _____
Paragraph 5: _____	Paragraph 5: _____

EXERCISE 7-6
Paragraph Writing:
Stipulated Definitions

Directions: Choose two of the words below and write a paragraph of definition for each one. Remember that you will be stipulating your *personal* interpretation of the meanings of the words. At the end of each of the paragraphs, indicate the type of development you have used.

1. Success
2. Humor

3. Friendship
4. Beauty
5. Responsibility
6. Masculinity
7. Femininity
8. Intelligence

8

FROM PARAGRAPH TO COMPOSITION

EXPANDING A PARAGRAPH

Thus far in this book you have been asked to practice certain skills which lead to the production of well-organized paragraphs, the basic units of composition in English. However, it is rare that you will be asked to write just one paragraph in isolation. Ordinarily, any writing task will involve a series of related paragraphs on a given topic—that is, a composition. If you are able to compose a logical, coherent paragraph, it will not be difficult for you to *expand* that paragraph into a longer composition in which you can more fully develop your topic.

How is this done? One possible method has been illustrated for you on the two pages which follow. Study these two pages carefully, then look over the explanatory chart on page 182.

MODEL PARAGRAPH 1

[1]Although African survivals in American culture have diminished over the past one hundred years, some are woven into the cultural pattern of America. [2]The words *tote* (to carry) and *juke box* have been taken directly from African languages. [3]One of the Negro's greatest contributions to American music, the spiritual, is a blend of primitive African music and the religious fervor of Christianity. [4]Foods such as okra, watermelon, and even coffee have their roots in Africa. [5]These everyday elements are astonishing evidence of the African contribution to American life.[1]

[1]Adapted from Romeo B. Garrett, "African Survivals in American Culture," *Journal of Negro History* (October 1966), Vol. 51, No. 4, pp. 239–245.

MODEL COMPOSITION 1

¹   African survivals in American culture have diminished markedly over the past one hundred years, but some are still existent and are interwoven into the cultural pattern of America and the Western Hemisphere itself. These are reflected in the words we speak, the songs we sing, and the foods we consume.

²   A recent work on Negro speech in the United States reveals more than four thousand African words, names, and numbers, still spoken among Negroes on the Georgia-South Carolina offshore islands, known as the Gullah region. These words reveal the identity, civilization, and relative influence of the people from whom most of America's twenty thousand Negroes descend. For example, the word *tote,* meaning "to carry," has been found in print within seventy years after the first settlement at Jamestown, Virginia; it has no known English origin. Our latest, *juke box,* comes from the word *juke,* a Senegalese term implying a wild time.

³   Negro spirituals, too, are traceable to Africa, and their identical prototypes can be found in African music. Once in America, these original patterns were fused with the spirit of Christianity, a religion which promised that in the next world the adverse conditions of the slave would be reversed. The result was a body of song voicing all the cardinal virtues of Christianity—patience, forebearance, faith, and hope—though a necessarily modified form of primitive African music. The Negro took complete refuge in Christianity, and his spirituals were literally forged out of sorrow in the heat of religious fervor; they brought hope and comfort to a burdened people.

⁴   Anthropologists attest that many of our most popular plants have their roots in Africa. Black-eyed peas traveled from Africa to North America in the holds of slave ships as food for the pitiful cargo. Africa's greatest contribution to the joy of eating is the watermelon, which is still found wild in the interior of Africa, where it originated. Our word *coffee* is derived from Kaffa, Ethiopia, its place of origin. *Okura* (okra) and *kola* nuts (the basis for cola drinks) were both brought to the new world by Africans.

⁵   These astonishing survivals of African culture prompted the late Professor Carter G. Woodson, one of the world's most eminent authorities on Negro culture and history, to state, "All around me I can see Africa. . . ."

Note the various relationships which exist between the paragraph and the composition:

Sentence 1

Sentence 2
(words)

Sentence 3
(songs)

Sentence 4
(foods)

Sentence 5

INTRODUCTION

Paragraph of introduction. In this paragraph the reader is given certain background information. The *controlling idea* of the composition is given in the last part of the paragraph, where the reader is introduced to the various topics of the paragraphs which are to follow: words, songs, food.

BODY

Paragraph 2 (words). This paragraph deals with African words which are still used in American English. It goes into *far greater detail* than the single sentence of the model paragraph.

Paragraph 3 (songs). The third sentence has also been expanded into a full paragraph, this time one which deals with the Negro spiritual.

Paragraph 4 (foods). This paragraph represents an expansion of the fourth sentence of the model paragraph. Like the others, it presents quite a bit more detail than is possible in a single sentence.

CONCLUSION

Concluding Paragraph. This final—or concluding—paragraph, like the final sentence of the model paragraph, ties together all of the ideas expressed in the composition. The composition ends with a *quotation*. This is a useful technique to learn, particularly for paragraphs of introduction and conclusion.

CONTROLLING IDEA VS. TOPIC SENTENCE

You will notice, from reading the preceding model composition, that the first paragraph is unlike any of the paragraphs which you have seen so far in this book. It is called a *paragraph of introduction.* The first thing you will notice about it is that it does not begin with a topic sentence; in fact, there is *no* topic sentence which applies to only that paragraph. Rather, its first sentence introduces the general idea of African survivals in the United States today. The second sentence is more specific: it narrows the choices down to *three* of these kinds of survivals—1) words, 2) songs, and 3) foods. We will call this sentence the *controlling idea* of the composition, since it announces in very precise fashion what is to follow. The next three paragraphs then talk about each of these kinds of survivals. They all have topic sentences; each topic sentence reminds the reader that one specific kind of African survival is being discussed.

We might say, then, that a controlling idea is *more powerful* and *more general* than a topic sentence. This is not surprising, since a controlling idea controls not a single paragraph, but rather an entire composition. It announces to the reader the main idea of that composition; any topic sentences which follow in subsequent paragraphs help to develop that main idea in much the same way that, in a single paragraph, each sentence helps to develop the idea announced in the topic sentence:

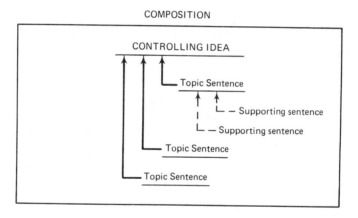

EXERCISE 8-1
Analyzing Paragraph Structure
in Relation to Composition Structure

Directions:

1. Carefully read Model Paragraph 2 and Model Composition 2, which follow.

2. Number each sentence of Model Paragraph 2 and each paragraph of Model Composition 2 in the same way as was done for the first model paragraph and model composition (pp. 180–181).

3. Draw arrows to indicate the sentence-paragraph relationships which exist.
4. *Circle the controlling idea* in the model composition.
5. *Underline the topic sentences* of the remaining paragraphs.

Then:

6. Construct a chart for Model Paragraph 2 and Model Composition 2. Use the chart on p. 182 as your model. You have no doubt figured out by this time that there is no paragraph of conclusion. Is there a conclusion at all? If so, try to locate it.

MODEL PARAGRAPH 2

Because Americans are a blend of people from many countries, there are only a few characteristics which can be applied to all Americans. Perhaps the most basic of these is American individuality, which is evident in our history from the days of our founding fathers. The second characteristic shared by all Americans is our paradoxical combination of idealism and practicality. Another typically American feature is the emphasis we place on money and the things it can buy—i.e., our materialism. Finally, in practically all American families, our parents exert less influence on us than do parents in other parts of the world. These elements are deeply embedded in the American character, but like many other things American, are subject to change in a relatively short period of time.[2]

MODEL COMPOSITION 2

WE AMERICANS

Since we Americans are a blend of people from many countries, we have a very short history which can properly be called "American." Therefore, it is hard to find characteristics which apply to all Americans. We combine many extremes from many different cultures. Nevertheless, we can make some generalizations. Our main characteristics include individuality, a combination of idealism and practicality, materialism, and a lack of parental influence, all of which permeate our lives.

[2]Gilbert D. Couts, "We Americans" (unpublished essay, American University, 1977).

We Americans value individuality. Our country was founded by strong individuals, and we do not like to be forced into conformity. Therefore, we insist on having a great deal of freedom. Interestingly enough, however, most Americans use this freedom to behave very much like most other Americans, and we are suspicious of those who do not conform. Hippies are individualists, for example, but most Americans do not like them. By the same token, we consider ourselves very faithful to the laws of our country, but there are few among us who would not break one if it was felt that no harm would be done by doing so—such as by exceeding the speed limit or failing to report informally-received cash income on tax forms.

Secondly, we Americans are both practical and idealistic. We place great value on doing things for ourselves, for this is what our pioneer forefathers were forced to do. Many foreign visitors are surprised to find that many couples of comfortable means do their own yardwork, their own housework, their own repairs. On the other hand, we are very idealistic: we think we have the best political, social, and economic system yet devised, and we therefore expect everything to go smoothly. As a result of our idealism, we are easily disillusioned. This is why so many marriages end in divorce—young couples' expectations from marriage are often unrealistically high. Similarly, it helps explain the dissatisfactions and protests of many young people, and even older people, who enjoy one of the highest standards of living in the world.

A third characteristic of us Americans is that money is more important than prestige to us. People work extremely hard, so many, unfortunately, either have little leisure time, or do not know how to enjoy it. Why do we work so hard? It is not to achieve greater status or prestige, but simply to have more of the material objects and comfort that money can buy.

Finally, our parents have less influence on us than parents do in other countries. Many children are left in day-care centers by their working mothers, or with babysitters when their parents go out at night. Furthermore, peer pressure is very great because children's feelings and desires are taken very seriously, and they are given a lot of freedom to form strong personalities. We leave home at a relatively early age, usually after high school, to take jobs and have our own apartments, or to go to college, where we are allowed a great deal of freedom. We choose our own spouses, even if our parents object. And, later in life, when our parents are old and helpless, we often live far away from them; many prefer to put them in nursing homes rather than to have the responsibility of caring for them daily. Many foreigners find this practice heartless. I suppose it is, but like many other qualities we Americans share, it is subject to change over a relatively short period of time.

MIXING METHODS OF PARAGRAPH DEVELOPMENT

You have studied the various methods of arranging supporting sentences (enumeration, process, chronology, cause-effect, and comparison and contrast). You have also seen that examples, details, anecdotes, and facts and statistics can be used with any of these methods.

In like manner, the methods themselves are often *combined* in a longer composition. A good writer will frequently make use of all or a number of these methods to develop his topic. For example, in one paragraph he may enumerate his supporting sentences in descending order; in the next, he may make use of comparison or contrast, quoting statistics to prove his point; another paragraph may use a cause-effect development.

EXERCISE 8-2
Identifying Types of
Paragraph Development
in a Composition

Directions: Reread the composition "We Americans." For each of the paragraphs, identify the type of paragraph development used. If you think that more than one method has been used in the same paragraph, indicate this.

Paragraph 1: <u>cause-effect, enumeration</u> _____

Paragraph 2: _____

Paragraph 3: _____

Paragraph 4: _____

Paragraph 5: _____

EXERCISE 8-3
Composition Writing: Enumeration

Directions: Expand the paragraph you wrote in Unit Three, Exercise 3-8— the qualities of a good husband or wife—into a full composition. Look over the guidelines below before you begin to write.

I. INTRODUCTION

You will have to expand your original topic sentence into a *paragraph of introduction.* Your controlling idea should be the last sentence of the paragraph. Study the paragraphs of introduction of the two model compositions in this unit to get ideas for your first paragraph.

II. BODY

You will want to devote one entire paragraph to each of the qualities you mention. Three or four paragraphs, each devoted to one particular quality, will be sufficient. You will, of course, have to go into greater detail for each of the qualities than you did in your original paragraph.

Arrange the paragraphs of the body in either *ascending* or *descending* order.

Be sure to begin each paragraph with a *topic sentence* that tells the reader which quality you will be discussing in that particular paragraph.

III. CONCLUSION

You will have to add a *paragraph of conclusion.* In it you should summarize, restate, or reemphasize the main ideas in your composition. Notice how the authors of both model compositions in this unit have used a single pronoun—*these*—to remind the reader of all the paragraphs in the body of the composition. You might want to try this technique. You might also want to use a *quotation.*

Note: Don't forget to indent!

EXERCISE 8-4
Composition Writing: Information Transfer

Directions: Study the graph on page 189 very carefully. Then write a five-paragraph composition based on it. Your general topic will be world population growth as it relates to the continuing development of civilization. Use the following plan to develop your composition, which will have a title.

I. Title: Population Growth through the Ages

II. INTRODUCTION

Think of an interesting way to introduce the composition. Conclude the paragraph of introduction with a controlling idea in which you announce the general topics you will discuss in the three paragraphs of the body. (Suggestion: You might want to come back to your controlling idea after you have written the body to see if your controlling idea is well thought out.)

III. BODY

Paragraph 2: General population trends from 8000 B.C. to A.D. 2000. Use chronological development in this paragraph. Support your topic sentence with statistics.

Paragraph 3: The rapid population rise between A.D. 1000 and A.D. 2000. Use cause-effect development. From your knowledge of history, explain why there has been such a rapid rise in population during modern times. Be specific.

Paragraph 4: World population between 8000 B.C. and A.D. 1000 *contrasted* with world population between 1000 B.C. and A.D. 2000.

IV. CONCLUSION

Summarize the ideas you have discussed in your composition.

EXERCISE 8-5
Composition Writing (Mixed Methods)

Directions: Write a full composition on one of the following topics. Refer back to the model compositions in this unit for ideas.

1. A survival from another culture in your society
2. Characteristics shared by the people in your society.

POPULATION GROWTH THROUGH THE AGES[3]

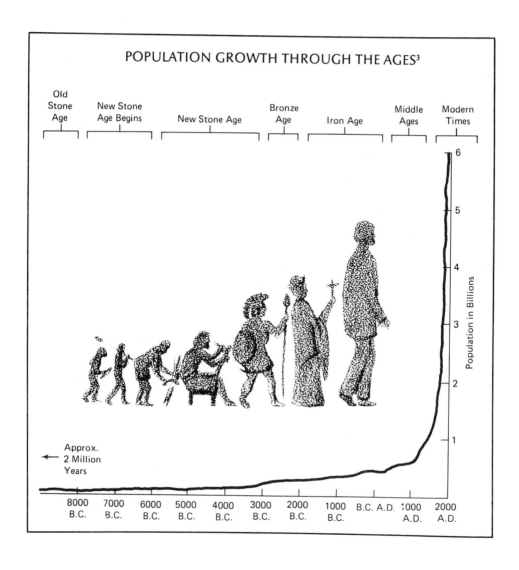

[3]Population Reference Bureau, *The World Population Dilemma* (Washington, D.C.: Columbia Books, Inc., 1972), p. 10.

INDEX